Praise for *A Restless Age*

"This is a swell book—if I do say so myself. (It's my translation that is privileged to supply the Augustine passages quoted in each chapter.) Austin Gohn shares my passionate hope that the *Confessions* will become as useful to Protestants as it has been to Catholics over the centuries. But as a writer he has important qualities I lack: he comes straight to the point in every discussion, and shows a virtuoso sympathy with young people in confusing, trying times."

> **Sarah Ruden,** Translator of Augustine's *Confessions* (The Modern Library, 2017)

"Few words are as synonymous with young adulthood as 'restless,' a vibrant adjective that is also forever associated with Augustine, who famously declared, 'our heart is restless until it rests in you.' It should be no surprise that young adults resonate with Augustine, if they take the time to read him. And if this book gets more of them to read Augustine, that's a win! Young adults need old, time-tested wisdom, especially in today's world of social media ephemera and soul-crushing digital delirium. Augustine is a good place to start, and *A Restless Age* tells us why."

> **Brett McCracken**, a senior editor at The Gospel Coalition and author of *Uncomfortable: The Awkward* and *Essential Challenge of Christian Community* and *Hipster Christianity: When Church and Cool Collide*

"In *A Restless Age*, Austin Gohn translates the ancient wisdom of Augustine to the modern twentysomething. In these pages you'll find a thoughtful, practical, and hopeful perspective on this important decade of life."

> **Drew Moser**, Ph.D. Professor, Taylor University, co-author, *Ready or Not: Leaning into Life in Our Twenties*

"Austin Gohn's *A Restless Age* cleverly merges the timeless concepts of Saint Augustine from the fourth century with current issues that young adults face in the twenty-first century. He gracefully challenges this generation to seek God for the elusive rest they need and provides relevant and practical ways to do it. It is an important read not only for people in their twenties but also those who live with, work with, and mentor them."

Vince Burens, President/CEO, CCO

"In this book, Austin Gohn gives us all a true gift. He creates an intersection between the long-standing wisdom of Augustine and the fresh experiences of a generation still coming into its own. There is truly nothing new under the sun, and this book helps every reader to bring long-standing realities to bear on new challenges. A worthwhile read for anyone searching for contentment, significance, and a deeply rooted journey with Jesus."

Casey Tygrett, speaker, author of *As I Recall:*
Discovering the Place of Memories in Our Spiritual
Life, and host of the otherWISE Podcast

"One of the biggest struggles for twentysomethings—for most of us—is making time for self-reflection in the midst of our hurried, on-to-the-next-thing lives. We're running on the outside and restless on the inside—just like Saint Augustine. With witty metaphors and a deep understanding of our cultural moment, Austin Gohn brings this ancient saint into our present struggles. *A Restless Age* normalizes our angst, but—most importantly—offers a way out of it. I hope the words of this book enter the hearts of young adults everywhere who need an exit from life's "treadmill" and a soft place to rest their heads."

Erica Young Reitz, founder and principal, After
College Transition, author of *After College*

"In an era where 'Confessions' conjures in the mind of young adults an award-winning album by Usher, Austin Gohn has reintroduced the relevance of Augustine's classic work, wrapped it in a relatable wisdom, and delivered it all with more than a small amount of wit. *A Restless Age* shows us there is an ancient answer to a problem that may not be as modern as we've made it out to be and points us to the God who's been calling us into his rest all along. This is the kind of book you'll revisit, giveaway, and bring up at dinner parties."

Kelsey Hency, Editor in Chief of *Fathom Mag*

"This is a wonderful book. Austin Gohn 'gets' Augustine and then gives Augustine to the twenty-something wondering why life hasn't turned out as expected. *A Restless Age* is rich in biblical insight, perceptive in cultural analysis, and grounded in truth that goes much deeper than today's headlines."

Trevin Wax, Director for Bibles and Reference at LifeWay Christian Resources, author of *This Is Our Time: Everyday Myths in Light of the Gospel*

"We live in a time where your twenties can often feel more unsettled (and unsettling) than ever. *A Restless Age* draws practical wisdom, guidance, and encouragement from an unlikely source: Saint Augustine's stormy, tempestuous early life. Austin Gohn expertly weaves Augustine's hard-won insights into an essential guide for making your twenties a decade of fullness, purpose, and hope."

Tom Lin, President/CEO of InterVarsity Christian Fellowship

A Restless Age

A Restless Age

How Saint Augustine
Helps You Make Sense
of Your Twenties

AUSTIN GOHN

FOREWORD BY WESLEY HILL

Gospel-Centered Discipleship

A Restless Age:
How Saint Augustine Helps You Make Sense of Your Twenties

GCD Books
Austin, TX

GCD Books is a ministry of Gospel-Centered Discipleship. Our purpose is to produce resources that make, mature, and multiply disciples of Jesus.

For more resources from Gospel-Centered Discipleship, visit us at GCDiscipleship.com/Books and follow us on Twitter @GCDiscipleship.

Front cover design: Laura Schembre of Copper Street Design (copper-streetdesign.com)
Back cover & interior design: Benjamin Vrbicek (benjaminvrbicek.com)

ISBN 13: 978-0692148297
ISBN 10: 0692148299

CONTENTS

WESLEY HILL

W hen I was in my twenties, it felt like I was riding wild horses, and I was hoping I didn't go over a cliff." That's how singer/songwriter Chaka Khan has described what, for many of us, is the most turbulent decade of our lives. Young adulthood is when we aim for the stars and fall splat in the mud. It's the time when we reach for love and sometimes find heartbreak instead (or in addition). Musicians and writers often talk about needing to "find their voice," and young adulthood is the time when we make that attempt for the first time, trading in childhood dreams and fears and postures for new ambitions and anxieties and performances.

The book you hold in your hands is born out of intimate familiarity with this wondrous and stress-inducing process. Austin Gohn has been unusually attentive to his own journey through his twenties. Plus, in his role as a pastor, he's helped shepherd others along the same road. He hasn't just survived or coasted through young adulthood on autopilot; he's paid attention to it, noticing its strangeness, its poignancy and complexity—and the way it yields gifts and opportunities despite its challenges.

More importantly, though, Austin hasn't only relied on his powers of observation to write about the quest to live well as a young adult. He's looked for trailblazers who have already completed their pilgrimage through young adulthood and can offer hard-won wisdom as a result. The primary pilgrim Austin points to in *A Restless Age* is Augustine of Hippo, the fourth-century Christian bishop who wrote a kind of prayerful autobiography about how God found him in his twenties and turned him into a believer. You may not think an ancient saint would have much to say that would help navigate a world with Snapchat and Pornhub, but *A Restless Age* will convince you otherwise. This book shows how Augustine's self-examination in his book the *Confessions* can still speak across the gulf of seventeen centuries. While he may not have had the option of Internet dating, Augustine knew the kinds of longings and phobias that lurk in every human heart, regardless of era or culture.

Although it's been almost a decade since I exited my twenties, I still recall with mingled happiness and grief my trip through those trying, stretching, enlivening years. I started to question the certainties of my childhood faith. I fell in love for the first time and lost my best friend. I moved away from home and tried to forge a new identity. Through it all, I never lost my hunger to find God—or to be found by Him. I wish I had had *A Restless Age* to read during those years, not only for its witty diagnoses of twentysomething angst and its "Oh, that's so true!" insights into what makes young adults tick but also for its generous, compelling introduction to a saint who could have helped me hold onto faith and maybe even thrive.

Whether you're just embarking on the path of young adulthood or you're in the middle of your hike wondering how to keep going or you're looking back with regrets as well as gratitude, I'll say about this book what Augustine heard a child's voice singing so many years ago in a garden far away: "Pick it up! Read it!" Your life, like Augustine's, might just be changed if you do.

Wesley Hill
Professor at Trinity School for Ministry
Author of *Washed and Waiting*, *Paul and the Trinity*, and *Spiritual Friendship*

THE SEARCH UNDER THE SEARCH

In yourself you rouse us, giving us delight in glorifying you, because you made us with yourself as our goal, and our heart is restless until it rests in you.

— Augustine, *Confessions* (1.1)

I have climbed the highest mountains
I have run through the fields
Only to be with you
Only to be with you
I have run, I have crawled
I have scaled these city walls
These city walls
Only to be with you
But I still haven't found what I'm looking for
But I still haven't found what I'm looking for

— Bono, age 26

S aint Augustine's Instagram would have been crushing it. He lived in Carthage, Rome, and Milan before he was 30—urban centers that would have made any Internet listicle of top ten cities for young adults. He was in a long-term relationship with a woman he loved. He had friends who were willing to stay up late and discuss the meaning of life. His professional network included cultural influencers who could get you on the phone with the emperor.

He attended lectures hosted by spiritual celebrities, engaged in dialogue with philosophical thought leaders, and frequented a church led by one of the most influential pastors of the fourth century.

Yet Augustine was restless. Anxiety was ripping up his insides as he tried to keep up with the demands of his high-pressure career. Some of his friends were messing up his life and other friends were proving to be less permanent than he had hoped. His somewhat manageable teenage hormones had morphed into an uncontrollable appetite for sex by his mid-twenties. With the help of not-so-subtle hints from his mom, he was starting to realize that his long-term relationship needed to end. And if all that wasn't enough to ignite a quarter-life crisis, he was haunted by the possibility that everything he knew was wrong.

A few years ago, Stanford University students popularized the phrase "duck syndrome" to explain their own experience with young adulthood. Not unlike ducks, they appeared to be gliding across the surface of life. It looked, thanks to carefully curated social media feeds, as if everything was easy and effortless. They had good friends, good grades, and good career prospects. Just below the surface, though, they were kicking their feet in an anxious frenzy trying to stay afloat. They were frustrated, depressed, and even suicidal. Not unlike Augustine sixteen centuries before them, they were far more restless than they allowed others to see.[1]

---

[1] A version of this introduction appeared in *Fathom Mag* in 2018. See Austin Gohn, *Fathom Mag*, "The Patron Saint of Young

Young and Restless

I spent my first five years out of college as a pastor for young adults. I tried to help them make sense of their lives as I tried to make sense of my own. I was trying to understand them with the hope that I might end up better understanding myself. I read widely on young (or emerging) adulthood, attempting to gain clarity about a season that is notoriously difficult to define.

Young adulthood is complex because it's both an age and a stage. As an age, it spans from around your high school graduation party until your early thirties. For most of that age range, until about your mid-twenties, your brain is developmentally lopsided. The front of your brain, the part that says, "Maybe we should make a pros and cons list before we do anything," is trying to catch up with the back of your brain—a never-ending party where everyone is saying, "You only live once, bro!"[2]

As a stage, young adulthood is a season of searching. It's when you begin to experience the process of *differentiation*, which basically means you stop riding shotgun while your parents drive your life and take the wheel for yourself.[3] The emotional umbilical cord is cut and you're free to explore the world, even if you still sit at the kids' table with your nieces and

Adulthood," October 15, 2018, https://www.fathommag.com/stories/the-patron-saint-of-young-adulthood.

[2] Meg Jay, *The Defining Decade: Why Your Twenties Matter—And How to Make the Most of Them* (New York: Twelve, 2012), 135–136.

[3] Gordon T. Smith, *Consider Your Calling: Six Questions for Discerning Your Vocation* (Downers Grove: Intervarsity Press, 2016), 57.

nephews whenever you come home for Thanksgiving. It's the Amish *rumspringa*, except it lasts for a decade instead of two years.

You're less certain about the certainties you've been told to believe your whole life and you start searching for answers in other places. You're starting new habits and quitting old ones as you try to figure out what kind of person you want to become. You're returning fewer and fewer text messages from the people with whom you cried while singing Vitamin C's "Graduation (Friends Forever)" at prom a few months earlier, and you're struggling to find where you belong in a new college, a new city, or even in your hometown—now "new" as well, because all the old familiarities have been stripped away from it. You're searching for love as you watch friend after friend get married, move in together, and have kids (and usually not in that order). You switch majors every semester as you start to realize that maybe you can't be—or don't want to be—whatever you always dreamed you'd be.

It's a high-pressure search, which makes your twenties as terrifying as they are exhilarating. Little choices you make in your twenties have consequences that ripple into your thirties, forties, and beyond. "With 80 percent of life's most significant events taking place by age 35," writes clinical psychologist Meg Jay in *The Defining Decade*, "as thirty-somethings and beyond we largely either continue with, or correct for, the moves we made during our twenty-something years."[4] She compares young

---

[4] Jay, *The Defining Decade*, xii.

adulthood to a plane speeding toward the end of a runway. Tiny directional adjustments at takeoff can mean the difference between landing in Honolulu or Juneau. Often, you don't realize that anything changed until you step off the plane in your thirties into a blizzard wearing an outfit appropriate for luau.

This kind of pressure means high highs and low lows. It's why Taylor Swift can sing, "When you're 22 you feel like everything will be alright," and Blink-182 can sing, "Nobody likes you when you're 23." It's why the infamous "27 Club" exists, which includes musicians like Amy Winehouse, Kurt Cobain, and Jim Morrison, who all died at the same age mostly due to suicides or drug overdoses. It's why your older friends will tell you not to waste your twenties.

If there is one word I've found that sums up young adulthood, it's *restless*. It's the feeling of thinking you've finally arrived at the party only to find out someone moved it to another location. It's the feeling of trying to keep up only to feel like you're falling further behind. It's the feeling of something poking your mental pressure points until you start to lose it. It's the feeling you try to numb away with seven straight episodes of your favorite show on Netflix. It's the feeling you think no one else is feeling. It's the feeling of searching for something without being exactly sure what you're searching for.

And it's a feeling as ancient as Augustine.

The Patron Saint of Young Adulthood

I had never heard of Augustine until my freshman year of college, unaware that my own name is actually a derivative of his. Augustine lived in the crease between two centuries (A.D. 354–430), a period of transition in which the lights went out on the Roman Empire and everything went dark. As a theologian and church leader, he preached more sermons and wrote more pages than you can imagine as he tried to make sense of both what was happening around him and what had happened within him. His *Confessions*, which explores the spiritual landscape of his pre-Christian life, "has been the single most read, reread, and quoted post-Biblical Christian book ever written."[5] For me, it was nothing more than required reading. I skimmed it, survived the discussion group, and stuck my copy on the shelf next to other books I would one day try to sell at a marginal discount to unsuspecting freshmen.

It was seven years before I read it again. I was in my first year of seminary and leading a small ministry to young adults. As I read it for the second time, I remember thinking, *Augustine could be someone in my young adults ministry.* I felt like I was reading the most relevant book about young adulthood I had ever read. He was asking the same questions as the young adults I knew, sharing the same fears and struggles, and worrying excessively about work and love. I didn't just feel like I was reading about the young adults at my church, though. I felt as if I was reading about myself.

For Roman Catholics, Augustine is the patron saint of sore eyes, vermin, brewers, printers, and

---

[5] Peter Kreeft, *I Burned for Your Peace: Augustine's Confessions Unpacked* (San Francisco: Ignatius Press, 2016), Location 90, Kindle.

theologians.[6] That means if you're the kind of person who prays to saints, you ought to ask Augustine for help when you've got pink eye or a rat problem (or, God forbid, *both*). Even if I do not participate in this tradition, I do believe he ought to be considered the patron saint of young adulthood. Before he was Augustine the saint, he was Augustine the twenty-something. Young adults everywhere should be wearing his medal.

Augustine wrote his *Confessions* about a decade after his conversion to Christianity, just as he was approaching middle age. After exploring his infancy and teenage years, Augustine spends most of its pages unpacking his young adult years, from his late teens through his early thirties. Some call *Confessions* a spiritual autobiography, but anyone who has read it knows that it defies any category. It reads like a memoir, a thriller, an exploratory essay, a philosophical treatise, a hymnal, a sermon, a love story, a devotional—all framed as a conversation with God. He meanders in and out of philosophical asides, quotes the Bible like it's going out of style, and often explodes into worship and praise.

In the opening section, Augustine writes a line that haunts the whole of his *Confessions* and the whole of this book, praying, "In yourself you rouse us, giving us delight in glorifying you, because you made us with yourself as our goal, and our heart is restless

---

[6] "Saint Augustine of Hippo," *CatholicSaints.Info*, last modified September 28, 2018, https://catholicsaints.info/saint-augustine-of-hippo.

until it rests in you" (1.1).[7] Although he introduces the book with this line, it's really more of a hard-won conclusion he discovered only after spending his twenties searching for rest in all the wrong places. On nearly every page, you can sense his spiritual anxiety as he tries one possibility after another, hoping to find what he's looking for. Only at the end of young adulthood did Augustine realize that what he was looking for was right in front of him all along.

In *You Are What You Love*, philosopher James K.A. Smith engages with Augustine's opening idea.[8] At our core, in what Augustine calls our *hearts*, each of us wants something we are often unable to name. It's an open-ended desire, a gravitational pull, a homing beacon, a motor that never turns off. "The longing that Augustine describes is less like curiosity and more like hunger," Smith writes, "less like an intellectual puzzle to be solved and more like a craving for sustenance." We're all searching for something to meet that desire, to satisfy our longing, to appease our craving, to give us rest. It's the search under the search for answers, habits, belonging, love, and work.

Within each of our hearts is an instinct similar to what allows a homing pigeon to find its way home. In a short documentary called *The Homing Instinct*, cameras follow the lives of two elderly pigeon-racers named Jackie and Maurice. They have been racing pigeons since the end of World War II, and every year they prepare for the big one: a lengthy race from

---

[7] Augustine, *Confessions*, Trans. Sarah Ruden (New York: Modern Library, 2017). In the rest of the book, I will mark each quote with a parenthetical reference to the book and section number.

[8] James K.A. Smith, *You Are What You Love: The Spiritual Power of Habit* (Grand Rapids: Brazos Press, 2016), 7–10.

Bourges, France, across the English Channel to their home in northeast England. Two days after thousands of pigeons are released from semi-trucks in Bourges, Jackie and Maurice stand looking to the sky waiting for their pigeons to come home. Jackie wins third place, which thrills him, but the documentary ends with Maurice still waiting for his pigeons to return home.

No one seems to agree on exactly how homing pigeons can find their way home. The sun, low-frequency sound waves, an intense sense of smell, and landmarks have all been suggested and debated by scientists. Jackie, who also has an opinion, thinks it's nothing more than a "highly developed instinct." This instinct is developed by using food and love to give the pigeons a strong sense of *home*, a process shown in the documentary, slowly letting them navigate back home from increasing distances.

Smith compares the search for rest to the buoyancy of a beach ball. If a beach ball is held under water, it cannot be at rest because the ball is trying to get to the surface of the water. When you let go, it rises to the surface where it belongs. Augustine compares the search for rest to fire, rocks, oil, and water in one paragraph, saying,

> A material object works its way toward its own place by means of its own weight. A weight doesn't simply direct its course to the lowest level, but to its own proper place. Fire moves up, stone down. These things are in motion through their own weights, and they seek their own places. Oil poured underneath water rises to the top, and water poured on top of oil sinks

underneath. They are set in motion by their own
various weights, to seek their own places. Things
that are not set in the order they should be are
restless; once set there, they rest. (13.10)

To be at rest, according to Augustine, is to be where
we were made to be. It's to find what we've been
searching for everywhere. It's to be rightly ordered.
It's to come home.

Rest is Augustine's shorthand for a sense of joy,
peace, happiness, or fulfillment that cannot be lost.
It's spiritually catching your breath. It's what Jesus
meant when he said, "Come to me, all who labor and
are heavy laden, and I will give you rest. Take my yoke
upon you, and learn from me, for I am gentle and
lowly in heart, and you will find rest for your souls.
For my yoke is easy, and my burden is light" (Matt.
11:28–30). It's what the ancient poet meant when he
said, "As a deer pants for flowing streams, so pants
my soul for you, O God" (Ps. 42:1). It's what God pro-
claims through the prophet Jeremiah, saying, "Stand
by the roads, and look, and ask for the ancient paths,
where the good way is; and walk in it, and find rest
for your souls" (Jer. 6:16). In Augustine's dictionary,
rest is not just a good nap on an old couch; it's discovering and reordering our lives around the One who
made us for himself.

The problem arises when we try to find rest in
other things, in things less than God, in things that
are always on the run. Most of Augustine's *Confessions* is the story of what happens when you search
for rest in all the wrong places. Like young adults today, he searches for rest in many of the same places
we seek rest: answers, habits, belonging, love, and

work. Over and over throughout the book, after coming up short again, he says things like this:

> My sin was that I sought not in God himself, but in things he had created—in myself and the rest of his creation—delights, heights, and perceptions of what was true and right, and in this way I collapsed into sufferings, embarrassments, and erring ways. (1.31)

> There's no rest where you're looking for it. Look for what you're looking for—but it's not there where you're looking. You're seeking a happy life in the land of death. It's not there. How can there be a happy life where there isn't even life? (4.18)

> Oh, the twisted roads I walked! Woe to my outrageous soul, that hoped for something better if it withdrew from you! The soul rolls back and forth, onto its back, onto one side and then another, onto its stomach, but every surface is hard, and you're the only rest. (6.26)

By looking for rest in all the wrong places, he ended up with everything except rest: pain, hurt, confusion, frustration, anxiety, fear. Whatever momentary rest he achieved in love, work, or anything else turned out to be nothing more than illusion.

Many of us are living in the tension that encompasses most of Augustine's *Confessions*. Some of us are tired and frustrated, worn out from spending our twenties searching for rest. We know Bono's lyric, "I still haven't found what I'm looking for," from experience. Others of us are still optimistic, thinking that the rest we're searching for is just around the next corner—one swipe, one click away. And still others of us have given up the search completely, opting to just live in the restlessness. Is there another option?

C.S. Lewis, in a sermon from 1941, considers the same feeling Augustine inhabited throughout the years he writes of in his *Confessions*. To those who feel like there's nothing in this world that can give them rest, Lewis writes, "Apparently, then, our life-long nostalgia, our longing to be reunited with something in the universe from which we now feel cut off, to be on the inside of some door which we have always seen from the outside, is no mere neurotic fancy, but the truest index of our real situation."[9] You're not crazy for feeling restless, he says. You're not crazy for thinking that every moment of love, joy, fulfillment, beauty and meaning is just a shadow of something else. It's possible, he says, that our rest-less hearts are a clue that we were made for something—or someone!—beyond this world, yet as close as our breath.

You were made for God, Augustine says. You were made to know him as he's been revealed in Jesus Christ. Only as you begin to structure your whole life around who he is, what he's done, and what he's said will you begin to experience the rest many of us spend our whole lives searching for. That's what this book is all about. Many of us spend our twenties looking *for* rest, but Jesus is inviting you to spend your twenties living *from* rest. That's the good news, the gospel. In-stead of searching for rest in answers, habits, belonging, love, and work, you can enjoy those things

---

[9] C.S. Lewis, "The Weight of Glory," *The Weight of Glory and Other Addresses* (New York: HarperOne, 2001), 42.

for what they are, having already found what you're looking for.

A Restless Age is organized around the five basic young adult searches: answers, habits, belonging, love, and work. In each chapter, we will unpack what that search looked liked in Augustine's life, what that search looks like in our cultural moment, and how the "gospel of the restless heart" meets us right where we are.[10] I am no expert on Augustine, but I have wrestled with him and been changed by him. I'll be using Sarah Ruden's fresh translation of *Confessions*, the translation that made me want to write this book, marking each quote with two numbers: the first being the book number (it's divided into thirteen "books" or chapters), the second being the section number. I suggest reading my book with some friends and using the discussion questions together. At the end of the book, there is an appendix with directions for developing your own sticky-note *Confessions* and another appendix with tips for how to read *Confessions*—even if you don't like to read.

I Hope This Book Sets You on Fire

In Book Eight of *Confessions*, Augustine meets with an aging but still influential pastor named Simplicianus. At this point, he was already convinced the gospel was true, but something—something he could not yet name—was holding him back. Hoping Simplicianus could show him the way out of this dilemma, Augustine poured out the details of his wanderings thus far.

---

[10] Kreeft, *I Burned for Your Peace*, Loc. 83.

I am certain Augustine was hoping Simplicianus would give him the solution to his problem, the step-by-step instructions for overcoming the resistance. Often, when young adults talk with men or women like Simplicianus, they want something similar. Instead of responding with a *solution*, though, Simplicianus told him a *story*. A story, unlike a solution, tiptoes past what C.S. Lewis calls the "watchful dragons" of the intellect and walks in the back door of our imaginations.[11] Augustine did not need more answers, more facts, more verses, or more reasons to believe; he needed a story that would set his imagination on fire, overcoming whatever hidden obstacles still remained.

Simplicianus opted for the story of Victorinus, a man who Augustine had mentioned earlier in the conversation. Victorinus had been a local celebrity in Rome when Simplicianus lived there. There was a statue of him in the Roman forum. Not unlike Augustine, he was a brilliant scholar. He was also an idol worshipper like much of the cultural elite at the time. Then, slowly, through conversations with Simplicianus—the same kinds of conversations Augustine was having—Victorinus began to believe. At first, afraid of what people might think, he kept his Christianity hidden from public view. Then, in a very public confession, he let everyone know that he believed the gospel. The moment would have been on par with a famous, atheistic philosophy professor from an Ivy

---

[11] C.S. Lewis, "Sometimes Fairy Stories May Say Best What's to Be Said," *On Stories: And Other Essays on Literature* (New York: HarperOne, 2017), 70. In particular, for Lewis, it was "fairy stories" but I believe the thought applies to many other stories as well.

League university professing faith in Jesus Christ in front of television cameras.

After hearing the story, Augustine says, "I was on fire for emulation—and that's of course why he told me the story" (8.10). Augustine wanted Victorinus' story to be his *own* story. He saw himself in the story and longed for his own story to end in the same way. Simplicianus knew this is what Augustine needed most—not a solution but a story.

I am no Simplicianus, but I hope that in this book you hear a story rather than another set of solutions. I hope that as you read vignettes of Augustine's story, as recounted in his *Confessions*, you begin to see yourself in them. I hope that, like Augustine after he heard the story of Victorinus, your imagination is set ablaze with possibility for what *could* be. I hope that wherever you find yourself in Augustine's story, you let his story carry you toward its gospel-filled ending.

SEARCHING FOR ANSWERS

I was, you see, holding my heart back from admission of the truth, as I feared the sheer drop into it; but hanging (myself) in the air above it was more like killing myself.

– Augustine, *Confessions* (6.6)

If belief was like a castle, I feel like I wandered out of it through a secret passageway in my early twenties and into the wide-open world of unbelief. Now, I might like to believe again, but I can't find the way back into the castle.

– Dylan, age 26[1]

E arly in my tenure as a young adults pastor, a friend invited me to a gathering of people with magical abilities. Since they were meeting in a state park surrounded by hundreds of tourists instead of a dark basement where no one would find me if my "invitation" was actually an invitation to be the yearly muggle sacrifice, I said, "Sure, sounds like a party."

---

[1] At the beginning of each chapter, I'll include a quote from Augustine and a quote from a young adult. Some of the young adults are well-known (e.g., Bono in the "Introduction" and Marina Keegan in "Chapter Three"). Others are young adults I've had conversations with while doing young adults ministry. Their names and ages have been changed.

When I arrived, I sat down in a circle of at least a hundred people, mostly young adults. In some ways, it felt like attending Pagans Anonymous, except instead of sharing our struggles we were sharing our supernatural powers through a bullhorn cranked up to ten. Some people shared traditional abilities like "fortune-telling" and "reading your mind." (If they could actually read my mind, they would know I was thinking, *Please no one ask me what I do for a living.*) Others shared more modern magical powers like rap, love, and poetry, and no one seemed afraid of being seen there—no one, except me.

It all reminded me of a similar moment in the life of Saint Paul. If you are unfamiliar with Paul, he was an early Christian missionary whose journeys are documented in a book called *Acts of the Apostles.* Once, when he had some time to kill in Athens, a group of philosophers and idol-worshipers invited him to a meeting at the Areopagus—not unlike the meeting I was attending in Pittsburgh twenty centuries later. He stood up confidently and said, "Men of Athens! I perceive that in every way you are very religious," before starting into an impromptu sermon on the one true God, complete with references to Greek pop culture.

As I sat there, dreading the arrival of the bullhorn and trying to come up with something to say, I started sweating a bit and wondering if this might be my "Paul at the Areopagus" moment. "Maybe," I thought, "I could tell them about how I have the supernatural power of the Holy Spirit and explain how they could each have that power as well!" I started formulating a tiny sermon outline (just in case!). As the bullhorn arrived, my confidence evaporated and I passed it to the four-year-old sitting next to me, who spoke confidently and eloquently of his own powers.

It was there, though, surrounded by a hundred twenty-somethings boasting of their magical powers, that I realized the complexity of the search for answers in our cultural moment. Here was a group of semi-pagans in the middle of an increasingly unbelieving and secular city full of church buildings left over from the previous century. For young adults today, searching for answers is not as simple as weighing the pros and cons of a traditional religion like Christianity against the pros and cons of total unbelief. On the contrary, there is a whole constellation of options somewhere in between the belief that characterized life a few hundred years ago and the unbelief of our present moment.

The search for answers is there, hidden in the background, creating a low-grade anxiety that marks everyday life in our twenties. If we could just find the right set of answers or the perfect advice, we think, then we could finally relax and get on with living. We feel the pressure of this search most when we get burned by the failed answers we didn't even know we were believing—when the person who promised to marry us walks away, when we lose a friend to suicide and have no way of making sense of it, when our debt-ridden college diploma cannot even get us a job as a barista. As Dallas Willard often says, reality is "what you run into when you are wrong."[2] Running into

[2] Dallas Willard, "Truth? Can We Do Without It?," *DWillard.org*, accessed October 8, 2018, http://www.dwillard.org/articles/individual/truth-can-we-do-without-it.

reality, like walking into a pole, hurts, but it tends us to wake us up from sleepwalking through our twenties and forces us to consider the possibility that we have no idea where to look for answers.

Cult Leaders, Skeptics, and Preachers

Augustine wanted answers. For him, the search for answers was a search for wisdom and truth. In his late teens, Augustine started to "seethe with enthusiasm for wisdom" (6.18) and, as a result, he experimented with the variety of religious options available to young Romans. Questions about the problem of evil and an ever-present fear of death formed a web of "viciously gnawing anxieties" (7.7) that pressured his search for answers. He wandered into a banned religious sect called the Manicheans, tried an early brand of skepticism, admired a philosophical system called Neoplatonism, and even dabbled in astrology—all before his thirty-second birthday.

Augustine grew up in a Christian-*ish* family with a churchgoing mom named Monica and a dad who stayed home on Sundays to watch the football game— or whatever Roman dads did on Sundays. Augustine knew at least the basic facts of Christianity and had a sense of how Christians would answer his questions about life and death. Once, when he was so sick he thought he might die, he asked that a Christian baptism be prepared for him (that is, until he recovered and changed his mind). At this point in his life, at least, he thought Christianity offered him nothing more than a get-out-of-hell-free card.

In his late teens, Augustine moved from the small town of Thagaste to the comparatively big city of Carthage, where he continued his education. It was there, free from the constraints of his mother's religion, that he discovered a fringe religious group populated by a cultured elite who had outgrown traditional Christianity. Some of their religious vocabulary would have sounded familiar, but they were using Christian words in novel ways. They were the Manicheans, and it was with them that he spent the next eight years of his life.

To a brilliant twenty-something like Augustine, the Manicheans were particularly attractive. His surface-level Christianity never stood a chance against Manichean marketing tactics. To an uncertain and wandering young adult, the Manicheans made "reckless promises of knowledge" (6.7). In response to his questions about God, the world, and the nature of evil, they promised an all-inclusive system that would, given enough time, make sense of everything. To the young Augustine, this seemed like the freedom he had been searching for his whole life.

The longer he spent with the Manicheans, though, the less convinced he was by their teachings. Describing this season of his life, he wrote, "Around eight years followed during which I rolled around in the mud of that deep pit and in the darkness of that lie, often trying to rise out of it but always taking a more forceful plunge back in" (3.20). Whenever he attempted to quit the cult, they sucked him right back into it. Even though he was growing disillusioned, the promise of eventual answers held him back.

Then, he met Faustus—the "Gilderoy Lockhart" of the Manicheans. If you are not familiar with *Harry Potter and the Chamber of Secrets*, professor Gilderoy Lockhart is a celebrity wizard who was far more impressive in his books than he was in person. When Harry, Ron, and Hermione finally meet him, he is a huge letdown. For Augustine, Faustus held the answers to all his lingering doubts about Manichean teachings. In person, though, Faustus seemed like nothing more than a religious salesman. After this experience, Augustine's faith in Manichean teaching as a source of answers was in "shambles" (5.13).

While he was still in the midst of the lengthy Manichean initiation process, he started consulting astrologers. Astrology promised that he could find the answers he was looking for in the alignment of stars and planets. Vindicianus, an older man whom Augustine trusted, told him to stop wasting "on that poppycock the trouble and attention that were needed for useful things" (4.5). You can make the stars say anything you want them to say. Despite warnings and repeated letdowns, Augustine kept an astrologist in his contacts list for the next few years.

Stuck in a cult he no longer believed in, Augustine spent his late twenties in a sort of spiritual no-man's-land. He was unstable, whipped around by religious cross-currents. As in a breakup with a manipulative lover, he carried this religious baggage around with him for the rest of his young adulthood. The Manicheans had welcomed him with promises of certainty, but they left him on the street more uncertain than ever before.

In a sort of religious rebound, he became enthralled with the Academics, a group that represented
the exact opposite of what had attracted him about
the Manicheans. Whereas the Manicheans had promised total certainty, the Academics promised only
doubt, saying, "They'd determined that no part of
truth could be grasped by humankind" (5.19). After a
bad experience with religion, doubt feels liberating.

Even doubt, though, did not seem to give him rest.
He felt stuck in a squishy middle, knowing that he
could not return to the Manicheans but also not feeling at home among the skeptics. Describing this
tension, he writes,

> Thus, in the tradition of the Academics (or what
> passes for it), I held all the possibilities in doubt
> and bobbed around among them all, but at least
> I decided to leave the Manicheans; I didn't think,
> even during what was a period of doubt for me,
> that I should stay in a sect I already felt was in-
> ferior to the teachings of many philosophers. Yet
> I absolutely refused to entrust the treatment of
> my soul's malady to the philosophers, since the
> health-giving name of Christ was missing from
> their works. (5.25)

These opposing pressures of doubt and belief pushed
him both into the back row of the local church and
into the philosophical literature of the Neoplatonists.

The Neoplatonists gave him a fresh fire for wisdom—a conversion of sorts—and he felt for a moment
that their philosophical arguments soothed his spiritual anxieties. It was the fulfillment of a seed planted
many years earlier while he was reading philosophy

as a teenager. As he listened to the preaching of Ambrose at the church he was attending, though, Augustine had the feeling that the Neoplatonists were still missing something. For a while, he continued to resist Christianity, saying, "I was, you see, holding my heart back from admission of the truth, as I feared the sheer drop into it; but hanging (myself) in the air above it was more like killing myself" (6.6). He was listening to Christian sermons, reading the Christian scriptures, and talking with Christian friends, but he opted for a space somewhere between Christianity and philosophy, a space that felt more akin to spiritual suicide than spiritual freedom. He was still searching for answers, but he held back from fully committing to Christianity.

Super-Novas, Super Burgers, and the Paradox of Choice

Even if you have never met a Manichean in your life, which I am almost certain you have not, Augustine's experience should feel familiar to you. Augustine spent his twenties in a state of spiritual anxiety searching for answers, wisdom, and truth. He could not shake the remnants of his childhood religion, still pushed on him by his mom. He was lugging around the spiritual baggage of nearly a decade with a less-than-Christian religious sect he discovered during the early years of life on his own—a religion which over-promised and under-delivered. His interest in the more "magical" option, astrology, had lost its allure in the same impulsive manner through which it came. Disillusioned, he rebounded into a relationship with the opposite of everything represented by his previous religious experiences: a philosophical outlook promised nothing but uncertainty. Still haunted by questions, he slipped into yet another brand of philosophy, which left more room for the possibility of certainty. And, in the midst of all this, he wandered back into his childhood religion on the weekends—if only to sit in the back row.

As I consider some of the young adults who have sat down in the back row of my own church with their arms crossed, or the young adults who have met me for coffee only to spill out their zigzag spiritual journeys, so many sound just like the twenty-something Augustine. Perhaps it's because our cultural moment has more in common with Augustine's world than the world of our great-grandparents.[3] We are living in what philosopher Charles Taylor calls a "spiritual super-nova,"[4] an explosion of options for how to make sense of your life.

It hasn't always been this way. A hundred years ago many were hopeful that science would one day be able to respond to many of the questions once answered by religion. As in the opening scene of *Indiana Jones and the Raiders of the Lost Ark*, it seemed possible to simply swap out the golden idol of religious answers for the sandbag of more scientific ones without the cave crumbling into chaos around us. Yes, there would always be pockets of superstitious folk, but for the rest of us, religion would eventually be

---

[3] This is basically the argument of N.T. Wright, *Spiritual and Religious: The Gospel in an Age of Paganism* (London: SPCK, 2017).

[4] Charles Taylor, *A Secular Age* (Cambridge: Belknap Press, 2007), 300.

edged out of our day-to-day experience, and the world would live happily ever after.

This is not what happened. The twentieth century proved that science alone is not able to provide "credible answers to the basic questions of life," as Dallas Willard argues in his book about spiritual knowledge.[5] In an article from 1999, the staff of *Newsweek* summarized "the deadliest century" for its readers:

> Europe will be glad to say goodbye to the 20th century. That is not how it was supposed to be. In 1900 hopes ran high. Science would put an end to deprivation and suffering. Electricity, railways and the telegraph were uniting the continent; nationalism and national conflicts would wither in the face of communications and economic progress. Modern weapons had made general war unthinkable. And in technology and philosophy, in literature, music and the fine arts, Central Europe was about to come into its own. Ours would be the German Century.
>
> Instead, Europe has been the killing field of our age. More people have been uprooted, imprisoned, enslaved, tortured and killed than in any comparable period in recorded history. Europe was the laboratory for two disastrous experiments in mass social engineering: communism and Nazism degraded and collapsed the grand

---

[5] Dallas Willard, *Knowing Christ Today: Why We Can Trust Spiritual Knowledge* (New York: HarperOne, 2009), 56.

projects of the 19th century to a rubble heap of disillusion and exhaustion.[6]

As a culture, we are waking up from this nightmare into a kind of hangover, which many refer to as the postmodern condition. Instead of asking ourselves what happened last night, everyone is asking what happened last century. The age of science left many disillusioned, empty, and still restless. While there are pockets of people who think this was nothing more than a hundred-year fluke on the upward path of progress and human potential, there are others who are beginning to realize that science might not have all the answers to our questions about life. It seems we must look elsewhere.

Our search is pressured on one side by a sense of restlessness and, on the other side, by a sense that there is no going back to traditional religions. We're trying to walk the tightrope between a way of seeing the world that leaves no room for anything beyond it and the feeling that we were made for something more than what the world offers. These different pressures created an explosion of options, of what Charles Taylor calls *third ways*.[7] Some of these third ways look like what I experienced in the park, and others hark back to the paganism of Augustine's own day. It feels like there are as many shades of belief and unbelief as there are people.

We are still asking many of the same questions, but there are no longer any default answers. If you

---

[6] "The Deadliest Century is Done," December 26, 1999, *Newsweek*, online, http://www.newsweek.com/deadliest-century-done-163268.

[7] Taylor, *A Secular Age*, 302.

have a question about the meaning of life or how to find a spouse, there is no clear sense of where you should look or whom you should ask. If you grew up in fourteenth-century Europe, you went to the priest. If you called Iraq your home, you might check what the Koran had to say. If you're trying to make it in New York City in the 21st century, you can ask Siri, Alexa, your mom, your friends, or a thousand others, and each will give you different answers to the same questions.

This is day-to-day life in the spiritual super-nova, which others might call an extreme brand of pluralism. Pluralism is about having more than one option for something. If you have ever been to an Eat'n Park (a local Pittsburgh late-night favorite) or a Denny's, you have experienced pluralism on a dietary level. The menu has more options than a person could consume in a few months of eating there. There are breakfast items, daily soup specials, salads (with fries on them if you're in Pittsburgh), a dozen kinds of burgers, some seafood, and a host of weekly pie options. There is something for every person of every taste in any mood at any time of the day. If Eat'n Park was monolithic, though, which is the opposite of pluralistic, the waiter would hand you a Super Burger instead of a menu and say, "This is what you're having." Sometimes I would prefer that.

In some ways, the rise of religious choices is a good thing. It means we can say that we no longer believe something just because our parents or culture believes it. In 2016, *The Atlantic* published a series of articles that chronicled the stories of young adults navigating all these religious choices, and in the opening article, Emma Green, a young adult herself, wrote, "Religion is no longer the mode through which many people live their lives, and this relatively new state of affairs affects even those who remain religious; it opens up the possibility of beliefs and practices that are not simply inherited but actively chosen."[8] Rather than naively accepting whatever is handed to us, we get to thoughtfully engage with the options we encounter.

But, as culture becomes more pluralized, many of us become more paralyzed. What originally felt like a wide-open ocean of opportunity can start to feel more like a tsunami of options threatening to drown us. Like pages being added to the already overwhelming religious menu, many of us find it more and more difficult to make a decision at all. If there are two choices, we can weigh the pros and cons of each. If there are three, we can consider more variables but still make a choice. If there are more than six or seven, we start to freeze up and hope someone will just hand us a plate of *something* so we can eat already. We are hungry, after all—that's why we're here.

Psychologists have a name for what you are feeling: the paradox of choice.[9] The more choices we have, the less able we are to choose. Our brains can handle only a small range of alternatives before shutting down. It is somewhat like the mental version of what happens to your computer when you open too many apps and the rainbow pinwheel of death signals

---

[8] Emma Green, "How Will Young People Choose Their Religion?," *The Atlantic* (Online), March 20, 2016, https://www.theatlantic.com/politics/archive/2016/03/how-will-young-people-choose-their-religion/474366/.

[9] Jay, *The Defining Decade*, 35–37.

that your computer might just shut down without warning.

Meg Jay, in her book on young adulthood, recounts a famous experiment that illustrates this paradox. Stanford researchers conducted a study in which two tables of jams were set up in a grocery store. One table had a mere six jams; the other, twenty-four. As customers sampled the jams at each table, they were offered a coupon for purchasing more of the one they liked. While the twenty-four-jam table attracted more attention, people were actually more likely to purchase a jam from the table with the smaller selection. Thirty percent of customers bought a jam from the small table but only 3 percent from the large table! That's the paradox of choice. Now, in addition to struggling to choose a religion, you will probably struggle to choose a jam next time you're at the grocery store.

Even if we manage to move our limbs and make a choice, we are haunted by the nagging demons of the other choices we could have made. And, often, those nagging demons are embodied in all the people we meet in everyday life. When we are surrounded by people who made different religious decisions than we did, we lose confidence in our own decisions, especially if they seem happier. We are constantly looking over our shoulders and asking, "What if I chose that instead? What if I made the wrong choice? Would I be happier and more fulfilled if I was a Buddhist?" In the end, we are a generation that is more indecisive than ever because we have more options than ever, and as we will see in the next chapters, this problem applies to more than choosing a religion.[10]

Faced with the overwhelming menu of religious options, many young adults are deciding not to decide. In a Pew Research Center study from 2012, researchers used the term "nones" to describe an increasing subset of twenty-somethings who do not associate with a particular religion.[11] In their study, they discovered that a third of adults under 30 are "religiously unaffiliated." Although some of them are atheists, many of these "nones" still consider themselves *spiritual* in some sense of the word. They are just not interested in getting too snuggly with any one brand of belief or unbelief. While there are many factors that contribute to this, the greasy fingerprints of the paradox of choice are all over it. In the end, we're plagued with indecision because it's just too hard to choose.

How the Paralyzed Start to Personalize

One of the side effects of the abundance of options is the rise of personalization: we expect that we should be able to customize just about anything. Like many young adults, I worked at three different coffee shops before the age of 25. It was common for customers to add so many adjustments to their order that by the time I made the drink it was a different drink entirely.

---

[10] Derek Rishmawy has a good discussion on this effect in "Ministering to Millennials in a Secular Age," *The Gospel Coalition*, January 23, 2018, https://www.thegospelcoalition.org/article/ministering-to-millennials-in-a-secular-age/.

[11] "'Nones' on the Rise," *Pew Research Center*, October 9, 2012, http://www.pewforum.org/2012/10/09/nones-on-the-rise/.

Instead of ordering a latte and leaving the rest to me, their preferences were piled into the order until it was a skinny, half-caff latte with a dash of chocolate syrup, two pumps of sugar-free vanilla, and milk that was steamed to *exactly* 135 degrees.

Even religion has not escaped the trend of personalization. What is true has become what aligns best with our personal preferences. Instead of choosing one set of answers, we mix and match ideas from different sources and build our own little religions—complete with their own saints, scriptures, and rituals.[12] Our saints might be Oprah or Jordan Peterson. Our scriptures might be anything by Elizabeth Gilbert or Tim Ferris. Our rituals might be meditating for thirty minutes in the morning or watching another episode of our favorite Netflix show before bed. In *The Impulse Society*, Paul Roberts describes this personalization of everything as rejecting "the world 'as is,' and instead [insisting] on bending it to our own preferences."[13] We are the captains now.

In an interview with thirty-something actor Andrew Garfield, Stephen Colbert asked him about his preparation for his role as a Jesuit missionary in the movie *Silence*. In response, he spoke positively about studying with Jesuit priests, learning the spiritual exercises of Saint Ignatius, practicing an extended fast from food, and even going on a weeklong silent retreat. Yet, in the midst of all his positive comments about Christianity, he explained his personal

---

[12] James K.A. Smith, *Desiring the Kingdom: Worship, Worldview, and Cultural Formation* (Grand Rapids: Baker Academic, 2009), 19–27.

[13] Paul Roberts, *The Impulse Society: America in an Age of Instant Gratification* (New York: Bloomsbury, 2014), 129.

unwillingness to commit to any one religion, his pan-theistic leanings (that God is *in* all things), and his belief in angels and demons as some kind of energy or metaphor—all to the applause of the studio audience. Despite his admittedly profound experience with Jesus, Christianity was nothing more than something else for him to fit into his own personal sense of how reality works.

For young adults like Andrew Garfield and our-selves, Jesus is tossed into the religious latte alongside everything else. We take his "top hits" and leave the stuff that doesn't resonate with us. We take "do not judge" (Matt. 7:1) but leave anything about Jesus returning to judge the world. We take "God is love" (1 John 4:8) but leave anything about God's wrath against sin. We take "love your neighbor as yourself" (Mark 12:31) but leave any guidelines about sexuality.

Then, we mix and match a few out-of-context soundbites from Jesus, a tweet from James Corden, some inspirational thoughts from the Dalai Lama, a vague *Star Wars*-esque sense of "the Force," a couple of Hallmark clichés like "be true to yourself" and "everything happens for a reason," and a lyric or two from *Frozen,* until we have a set of answers that is just right for us. Even if most of us have never written these answers down, they are playing in the back-ground of our lives and shaping the choices we make.

As liberating as customization feels, it has failed to give any sense of the certainty that would enable us to live confidently. Many of us feel haunted by the fear that maybe we chose the wrong answers. Some of the answers we chose in our early twenties or as teenagers have turned out to be flat-out inconsistent with reality. We're still restless and, in the midst of this, some of us are wandering toward the churches we left after high school or never attended in the first place.

One of my friends grew up Catholic but slowly grew "disillusioned with the ritualistic stuff" and the dogma. Like many, he cannot nail down the exact moment he stopped believing, though he knows it happened sometime in his early twenties. As he moves into his thirties, though, he often finds himself craving the belief he has lost. In moments of boredom or monotony, he feels a lack of significance and meaning, a kind of flatness to his life. He says, "I start asking questions like: What's the point of all this? Am I just going to work this job day in and day out for the rest of my life and then die?" Even as he attended church for a season, he felt like he could not find his way back into his childhood belief.

In a similar vein, Augustine had a moment in his early thirties, after over a decade of following his religious curiosity wherever it led, when he lamented to his friends Alypius and Nebridius, saying,

> To hell with all this! We've had enough of this empty worthless stuff. We need to devote ourselves solely to investigating the truth. Life is wretched, and we don't know when death is coming. It can creep up suddenly. In what condition will we go out of this place? Where is it that we'll have to learn what we should have done when we were here? And, what's more, will there be penalties to pay for not doing it? (6.19)

My friend felt the pressures of insignificance and meaninglessness, while Augustine felt the pressure created by the fear of death and what comes next. When you're tired of searching for answers in other places but struggle to return to a traditional religion like Christianity, what are you supposed to do?

Jesus is Not the Answer

In the ancient city of Colossae, people were also mixing Jesus with answers from other religions and philosophies. They had already heard the gospel once (Col. 1:23), but, at some point, they wandered into a set of answers that looked less like Christianity and more like the cultural trends around them. They believed the "plausible arguments" (Col. 2:4) of the latest podcasts and TED Talks. They were captivated by the "philosophy and empty deceit" (Col. 2:8) that they heard from scholars at the local colleges and universities. They bought book after book of human teachings that had the "appearance of wisdom" (Col. 2:23), only for the books to end up at local used bookstores alongside other books that had, at some point, appeared wise too.

It was into this world, a world similar to both Augustine's and our own, that Paul wrote his letter to the Colossians, one of the letters included in the Bible. It is a letter dripping with the gospel, the good news about Jesus, to a community that felt like the gospel was not enough anymore. It is a letter that points beyond simplistic answers to the one who offers us something more than answers. It is a letter for those attending the magical gathering at the park. It is the letter our generation needs to read.

First, Paul makes the uncomfortable claim that "all the treasures of wisdom and knowledge" are hidden in Jesus (Col. 2:3). That was a bold claim in the Greco-Roman world, which had deities on every corner. It might be even bolder in our own world where claims like that are dismissed as intolerant or even extreme.[14] Instead of giving in to the cultural pressure to say *some* instead of *all*, Paul points to Jesus and says, *everything you need is there.* Look no further than Jesus. He has all the answers we need to live and die well. Unless we are convinced of this, we will always be prone to search for answers elsewhere.

There's a song by a band called Housefires that says, "I've seen many searching for answers far and wide / And I know we're all searching for answers / only You provide." This is what Augustine was starting to realize during his own search for wisdom, and what so many young adults begin to realize even if they do not yet have language to describe it. Near the conclusion of Book Six of *Confessions*, Augustine wrote, "Oh, the twisted roads I walked! Woe to my outrageous soul, that hoped for something better if it withdrew from you! The soul rolls back and forth, onto its back, onto one side and then another, onto its stomach, but every surface is hard, and you're the only rest" (6.26). We search everywhere for rest, but until we look to Jesus, we will always be tossing and turning in spiritual anxiety.

Second, Paul says that we cannot separate Jesus from his answers. He writes, "Therefore, just as you

---

[14] Gabe Lyons and David Kinnaman, *Good Faith: Being a Christian When Society Thinks You're Irrelevant and Extreme* (Grand Rapids: Baker Books, 2016), 39–47.

received Christ Jesus as Lord, so walk in him, rooted and built up in him and established in the faith, just as you were taught, abounding in thanksgiving" (Col. 2:6–7). In other words, we cannot receive the answers Jesus gives without first receiving the person Jesus is. His answers are only true if he is also Lord. Everything Jesus tell us about how to live is rooted in the fact that he is Lord over everything, the one to whom the whole world owes allegiance and obedience (Col. 1:15–20). Jesus and his answers are a package deal. We must reorder our entire lives around who he is, what he's said, and what he's done.

Culturally, we are okay with the possibility that Jesus is a helpful moral teacher. Even Augustine could see this, writing, "My understanding of the Anointed, my Master, was limited to the following: that he was a man of outstanding wisdom, and that no one could be his equal" (7.25). If we do not believe Jesus is Lord, though, none of his teachings mean anything. If Jesus is not Lord, what he says about loving your enemies is meaningless. We're better off defending ourselves at any cost. If Jesus is not Lord, what he says about serving the poor makes no sense. We're better off making sure we're taken care of. No matter how nice or logical these things feel, they are nonsensical apart from the fact that Jesus is Lord. It's all or nothing.

In an unsettling paragraph from *Mere Christianity,* a classic for those struggling with Christian belief, C.S. Lewis poses the problem like this:

> You must make your choice. Either this man was, and is, the Son of God, or else a madman

> or something worse. You can shut him up for a fool, you can spit on him and kill him as a demon, or you can fall at his feet and call him Lord and God, but let us not come with any patronizing nonsense about him being a great human teacher. He has not left that open to us. He did not intend to.[15]

Jesus cannot be personalized or mixed with other teachings from other sources. We can try, but in the end Jesus cannot be reduced to a list of answers to our nagging questions. He is not a god we can manage or an animal we can tame. Everything he said depends on everything he is.

Finally, Jesus is more than just another set of answers. This is what makes Jesus different from everything else on the religious menu. Jesus came because we needed something more than answers, because answers were not enough, because answers might be helpful, but they cannot heal. Jesus came to give us rest for our souls (Matt. 11:28–30). He did not live, die, rise again, ascend to the right hand of the Father, and promise to return for us one day just so we could have more answers. Jesus lived, died, rose again, ascended to the right hand of the Father, and promised to return one day because we needed a savior to rescue us from the failed answers of this world and deliver us into a kingdom where he reigns as Lord. It's a kingdom where we're permitted to ask hard questions about lingering doubts and a kingdom

---

[15] C.S. Lewis, *Mere Christianity* (New York: HarperOne, 2001), 52.

where we'll find answers to questions we never even thought to ask.

Earlier in his letter to the Colossians, Paul described this kingdom, saying that God "has delivered us from the domain of darkness and transferred us into the kingdom of his beloved Son, in whom we have redemption, the forgiveness of sins" (Col. 1:13–14). *This is the gospel.* More answers could not save us from the disaster of sin and death. More answers cannot help someone who is locked in a prison. We need someone from the outside to unlock the door and set us free. Jesus is not just "the answer," as popular bumper stickers are prone to say. He is something far more.

Answers alone cannot give us the rest we long for. Only Jesus, the one who came to bring us something more than another set of answers, can give us what we need. When Augustine was studying works of philosophy, which are full of many *true* things, he knew that the answers he found could not take him all the way to what he was searching for. They were missing something; they were missing Jesus (7.27). Like many of us, he knew this in his head, *he wanted to believe*, but he still struggled to give his heart over to it. It wasn't until a life-changing experience in a friend's garden that he was finally able to surrender.

SEARCHING FOR HABITS

I marveled that now I loved you, and not an appa-
rition in place of you. But I didn't stand still to enjoy
my God. I was ravished into your presence by your
beauty, but soon torn away from you by the weight
of myself, and I smashed down with a groan into
the lower things I've been writing of. The habits of
my body comprised that weight.

– Augustine, *Confessions* (7.23)

I feel like I can't write or create or do anything unless I take a few pills to numb my mind. I want to
change, but I feel like I can't change. In the morning, I resolve to do better but by the end of a long
workday, my passion is gone and the cycle restarts.

– Emily, age 27

I n one of the defining experiences of his childhood, Augustine stole pears. In one of the
defining experiences of my own childhood, I stole
pogs—round, cardboard advertisements used to play
a game that almost no one knew how to play.

My second-grade obsession with stealing pogs began with stealing a twelve-pack of crayons as a first-
grader. While the class was at recess, I took another
student's crayons out of his desk, broke them in half,
and threw them in the garbage. It wasn't that I needed
crayons; I already had a sixty-four pack with a built-

in sharpener. Something in me wanted to steal them, and I liked how it felt to steal something and get away with it. To make the sin even worse, I volunteered to help that student find his crayons later that afternoon, being particularly careful to lead him everywhere but the trash can.

When pogs hit their peak in the mid-'90s, I started stealing them from my closest friends. It wasn't because I needed pogs; it was because I enjoyed the act of stealing. As the thrill of stealing from friends faded, I decided to go big and steal pogs from a store called Christian Supply. While my parents were purchasing Bibles, I stuffed every pocket in my neon winter coat with dozens of pogs that said things like "God Loves You" and "Just Say No to Death and Hell" and "You've Got a Friend in Jesus." I almost got away with it, too, but my mom spotted a bright orange pog container sticking out of my pocket while we were out for pizza afterward.

In the show *Arrested Development*, George Bluth used a one-armed friend named J. Walter Weatherman to creatively scare his children out of bad behavior. My dad didn't have a one-armed friend, but he did know a police officer. One afternoon when I came home from the park with my friend Christian, I saw a police car parked in the driveway. As I walked inside, my dad told me that the police were here to talk with me about what I had stolen. A large, terrifying police officer with handcuffs in his hand sat me down and asked, "How would you like to spend a night in jail?" In the end, he gave me one of those police badge stickers, and I never stole anything again. That was also the last time I saw my friend Christian.

Augustine says that sinful habits tend to grow with us (1.30). If my dad hadn't scared stealing out of my second-grade self, I often wonder if that habit would have grown with me into my teenage years and possibly even into adulthood. Similarly, a little bit of pornography in your teens can wreak havoc on relationships in your twenties. A little bit of cheating in college can morph into messing with the numbers at your first job. A little bit of unchecked, senior-year ambition can turn into a monster that eats all your relationships, hobbies, and virtue.

There are those of us who spend our twenties trying to change our habits, and there are those of us who spend that decade trying to make peace with our habits. Some read everything they can on how to change, while others surround themselves with people who tell them to never change. Both sides are searching for rest, hoping to find it either in changing habits or in staying the same, yet many of us—no matter which strategy we choose—still feel restless. No matter how much we change, we feel like there's something within us that remains unchanged. No matter how much we affirm ourselves, it still feels like there is something within us that needs to change.

Augustine vs. Augustine

The habits we start in our teens are the habits we solidify in our twenties, until they become the habits we're stuck with in our thirties. Long before there was neuroscientific data to support this claim, Augustine knew about habits from experience. What had been a socially acceptable habit when he was fifteen became the focal point of an intense struggle in his early thirties. His reflection on it is the most compelling section in his *Confessions* and one of the most memorable in all of classic literature.

In a pre-Internet age, long before unlimited access to pornography, Augustine developed the kind of lust that dads of teenage sons tend to write off as natural, boys-will-be-boys behavior—especially in the fourth century. It began with a look here and there, an experiment or two with his newfound sexual attraction, but it quickly and recklessly grew into "a whole grove of shady love affairs, several species of them" (2.1). He went from feeling like he was in control of his sexual desire to feeling hijacked and out of control. It would have been easy to tear up these "thorn bushes of desire" by the roots when they were still small, but now they had grown "higher than [his] head," thicker than the chainsaw of his will could cut through (2.6). It's always easier to pull up a sapling than to chop down a tree. His mom warned him about the consequences of his habits, but what teenage boy is going to take his mom's advice about sexuality? Not Augustine, especially when his dad was high-fiving him for the changes his body experienced as a teenager. It wasn't long before his "lunatic lust" (2.4) began to wreak havoc on his search for love—a search we'll return to in chapter four.

Even after Augustine began to believe the claims of Christianity, he discovered that he was unable to resist the gravitational pull of over a decade's worth of habitual lust. Speaking to God, he writes, "I was ravished into your presence by your beauty, but soon torn away from you by the weight of myself, and I smashed down with a groan into the lower things I've been writing of. The habits of my body comprised that weight" (7.23). There was a gap between the life he thought he wanted to live and the life he was actually living, a gap between the habits he wanted to start and the habits in which he felt stuck. His mind was convinced by the truth of Christianity, but his heart was held back by the half-truths of *Sports Illustrated: Swimsuit Edition.*

In Book Eight of *Confessions*, "the story of how [God] broke those chains" (8.1), Augustine took a scalpel to his soul in a desperate attempt to make sense of his struggle. Here's what he discovered:

> The enemy possessed *my* wanting, and from it he had constructed a chain for me and con-stricted me in it. Inordinate desire arises from a twisting of the will; and in the course of slavery to this desire, a certain inevitability emerges. With these links, as it were, interconnected (and that's why I've called this a chain), a harsh slav-ery held me tightly in check. (8.10)

Instead of finding two equal and opposite forces at work within him, as the Manicheans had taught him to believe, he found in himself a single, *twisted* will. His wanting was "inordinate" or unregulated. It was desire gone wild. Given enough time, this desire, which once felt wild and free, transformed into a kind of house arrest anklet. What Augustine once did con-sciously, he now did without thinking. What he once did by choice, he now did automatically. He had be-come a slave to the thing he once freely enjoyed, even if the freedom was mere "fictional liberty" (3.16).

The closer he approached new habits, the more his old habits fought against him. It felt like waking up in the morning only to find your body stuck in a kind of sleep paralysis, resisting everything your brain is telling it. Augustine explains it like this:

> There's no one who'd like to sleep forever, and everyone with unimpaired judgment prefers being awake, yet a person generally puts off rousing himself while a heavy sluggishness lingers in his body, and he'd rather grasp at dozing—though by now he disapproves of it—in spite of it being time to get up. In the same way, I was quite convinced that it was preferable to give myself over to your loving care than to give in to my own inordinate desire, but whereas what won out in my mind proved better, the whim was my fetter. (8.10)

Even though he knew what better habits were, Augustine opted instead for the snooze button, saying things like *in a minute* and *let me alone a little while*.

Later, after hearing the story of Saint Anthony's conversion, Augustine suddenly felt as if he was face to face with the habits that were ruining his life. He could no longer put these habits out of his mind. He threw himself into the garden outside the house where he was staying, sobbing over his inability to change. Yet, at the same time, he was afraid of what life without these habits might be like, afraid of what might happen if God actually destroyed his chains. He only half-prayed, saying, "Give me chastity and self-restraint, but don't do it just yet" (8.17). His "ruthlessly impinging habits" kept whispering lies like

Are you really going to show us the door? and *Do you imagine you can make it without these guys?* (8.25). He would say things like, "Okay, right now, I'm letting it happen, right now I'm letting it happen," only to find that nothing happened (8.25).

Augustine wanted to change *and* didn't want to change at the same time. He wanted to start new habits, the habits associated with Christianity, but he was still holding onto the habits of his old way of life. He writes, "I myself, when I was weighing whether to serve God my Master (as I had decided to do long before), I was the person who wanted that and the person who didn't want that: it was simply me. *I didn't fully want it or fully not want it.* Thus I was inwardly at war and being laid waste by myself; yet this devastation was happening against my will" (8.22). In the end, it was "myself versus myself," Augustine *versus* Augustine (8.27). He was restless and at war with himself, trying to achieve new habits that were just out of reach, unable to find the rest he hoped would come if he could just change himself.

Naming Your Loops

Where Augustine spoke of a chain, modern-day brain experts might speak of a neurological phenomenon called *chunking.*[1] It's the process through which your brain says, "Every time he does that action, he tends to do this action next. Let's just make that automatic so he doesn't waste any more mental energy." If every time you walk into your apartment, you take your

---

[1] Charles Duhigg, *The Power of Habit: Why We Do What We Do in Life and Business* (New York: Random House, 2012), 17.

shoes off and start scrolling through Netflix, your brain will eventually *chunk* those actions together—forming a kind of chain. Or, whenever you're in line or stuck in traffic, you get on your phone and refresh Instagram seven times, your brain will *chunk* those actions into a habit. What begins as a conscious decision to scroll through Netflix or Instagram eventually turns into something you do without thinking.

The process of chunking is only magnified during the season of life that extends from your awkward puberty years until your mid-twenties. During this period, you're in what psychologists call a *developmental sweet spot*, which your brain hasn't experienced since you were a toddler and will never experience to the same degree again. Your brain is wiring and rewiring itself, chunking and de-chunking, making it easier than ever to start new habits and quit old ones. Meg Jay, explaining the young adult brain, says,

> Because our twenties are the capstone of this last critical period, they are, as one neurologist said, a time of "great risk and great opportunity." The post-twenty-something brain is still plastic, of course, but the opportunity is that never again in our lifetime will the brain offer up countless new connections and see what we make of them. Never again will we be so quick to learn new things. Never again will it be so easy to become the people we hope to be. The risk is that we may not act now. In a use-it-or-lose-it fashion, the new frontal lobe connections we use are preserved and quickened; those we don't use just

waste away through pruning. We become what we hear and see and do everyday. We don't become what we don't hear and see and do everyday. In neuroscience, this is known as "survival of the busiest."[2]

You can still change your habits after your mid-twenties, of course, but your brain is far more likely to be on your side in your early twenties.

Habits, both good and bad, work on a three-step loop.[3] First, there's a *cue*, which is a kind of mental trigger that says, "Turn on the habit machine, now." Using the examples from above, a cue might be the feeling of being exhausted after a long day of work or the feeling of being bored for more than a few seconds. Second, there's the *routine* itself. The routine might be watching another episode of something or looking at your high-school best friend's life through a filter on social media. Finally, there's a *reward*, which is what you get for finishing the routine. A reward might be the feeling of forgetting about how much you hate your job or the spike in mental pleasure you get when you check the red notification bubbles on your phone. These little rewards help our brains decide, "Let's make this habit loop permanent. I like how it makes me feel when it's over." In the end, hamster wheels like these make sense of nearly half of the actions we take in a day.

Some of these loops make our lives easier and better. If I had to think about tying my shoes every single time I was trying to leave the house, I would buy a

---

[2] Jay, *The Defining Decade*, 142.
[3] Duhigg, *The Power of Habit*, 3–30.

lifetime supply of slip-ons. On the other hand, there are loops that are wrecking our lives even if, at first, these loops felt innocent and fun. One of the loops that was wrecking Augustine's life was lust. In our own era, Augustine's loop might look like the habit of opening an "incognito window" on your Internet browser whenever you're bored and alone. What once left you feeling good when it was over now leaves you with an intensified version of the regret you feel when you eat Taco Bell at one in the morning—for the second time this week.

Each of us could name our own habit loops. There's the loop of making up lies whenever your parents or friends ask you how things are going. There's the loop of spending a quarter of your paycheck on clothes at Target when you intended to just get a gallon of skim milk. There's the loop of mentally quitting one of your college classes because you failed one quiz early in the semester. There's the loop of drinking a few Blue Ribbons whenever you're hanging out with new friends just to get the conversation going. There's the loop of popping a few pills whenever you're trying to fall asleep or trying to get work done. The list goes on and on. These are the loops that feel more like the chain Augustine described in his *Confessions*.

Craving is what makes the loop spin.[4] Many of us have experienced this craving in relation to food. The more boxes of Cap'n Crunch you eat, the more likely you are to crave other foods loaded with sugar. The more kale you eat, the more likely you are to desire other healthy, organic foods (and to look down on the

---

[4] Ibid., 31–59.

rest of us who still eat Cap'n Crunch like a herd of heathens). The same is true with every other habit we have. Our brains and our bodies gain an appetite, a kind of palete, for certain kinds of rewards. The more we satisfy a particular craving, the more likely we are to crave that reward more and more.

This sense of *craving* is what Augustine described using the term *desire*. Hidden within every habit is something we *want*, something we have taught our bodies to crave. For this reason, James K.A. Smith, working from Augustine's paradigm, says, *you are what you love*.[5] To love something is to want it—an ancient sense of the word lost on those of us who came of age with rom-coms like *Love, Actually*. Love is hardwired desire, not simply a magical feeling that comes and goes as it pleases. We *love* the reward at the end of the habit loop, and we build self-reinforcing habits that take us toward what we love.

If habits are loops of love, what do we do when we no longer love our loops?

To Change or Not to Change

If you browse the shelves at a used bookstore, you'll find a dozen books from *The New York Times* bestseller list a year earlier telling you either how to change or why you shouldn't change—each with their own celebrity endorsements. There are those who say *you'll feel at rest when you stop trying to change yourself*, and there are those who say *you'll feel at rest when you change yourself like the rest of us*. None of the experts seem to agree on how to change our

---

[5] Smith, *You Are What You Love*, 10.

habits or, even more vitally, whether we should change at all. To change or not to change, that is the question.

When *Frozen* was released, "Let It Go" was the creed for ten-year-old girls everywhere. It's one of those songs that worked its way into our cultural subconscious before many of us had even seen the movie. The more I heard the song, though, the more I began to wonder about what kind of life Queen Elsa is advocating—especially when, as a grown man, I began to hum the song to myself. When Elsa decides she is tired of trying to resist her whatever-you-touch-turns-to-ice powers, she sings,

> It's time to see what I can do
> To test the limits and break through
> No right, no wrong, no rules for me
> I'm free!
> Let it go, let it go!

According to Elsa, the real problem is not her inability to change but the pressure she felt to change in the first place. If this is the problem, then the answer is to quit worrying about what others will think and be the person she was always meant to be.

While the context of the movie seems to be a Nordic country in the nineteenth century, this song feels way more like an expression of a particularly American and modern ideology about human nature. In fact, it sounds like Lady Gaga's "Born This Way" from 2011 in which she sings,

> Don't hide yourself in regret
> Just love yourself and you're set

I'm on the right track, baby
I was born this way

For Elsa, Lady Gaga, and a chorus of others, you are fine just the way you are. Express yo'self. No one can tell you what you can and can't do. Kill the inner critic. The greatest sin is not being true to yourself. Everyone else can deal with it.

Yet, as new as this perspective feels, it's nothing more than an ancient Christian heresy recycled and rebranded for another age. In the earliest centuries of Christianity, there was a stream of belief known as *antinomianism*. *Anti* means *against* and *nomos* means *law*. Slap them together and you get *antinomian*, which is someone who says, "No rules for me!" While there are key differences between ancient antinomianism and modern self-expression as to the reasons for refusing to change, the result is basically the same: *you're fine just the way you are, #dontjudgemebro*.

As young adults, we're living in the aftermath of a culture that adopted this perspective, and many of us are starting to feel like it's not true. Anyone who tells a recovering alcoholic or someone struggling with a pornography addiction to "just let it go" is a terrible friend. I've talked to people who were told to just be themselves in their twenties and are still dealing with the consequences in their sixties. Despite the mind-numbing catchiness of Elsa's anthem, "letting it go" ends up wrecking her own life, the lives of everyone she loves, and her entire culture. C.S. Lewis, in what feels like commentary on this song, writes, "The most dangerous thing you can do is to take any one impulse of your own nature and set it up as the thing you ought to follow at all costs."[6] Just being yourself might not be the best thing for yourself or your society and, at its worst, it might cause an eternal winter to fall upon your Nordic kingdom.

Our credit cards are also telling a different story than the one we tell (or sing to) ourselves. We spend billions of dollars on diets, gym memberships, pills, therapy, and books every year trying to "revolutionize" our lives—the very lives we are so desperate to affirm. No matter how much we affirm ourselves, it feels like something within us is rejecting all the affirmation. Many of us have the unnerving sense that something about us is rubbing against the grain of the universe, and it's giving us splinters.

If we can't find rest in keeping the same habits, maybe we can find rest in changing our habits. Despite the cultural chorus telling us we're fine, it seems like everyone in our lives is making a host of improvements to themselves and taking meticulously angled pictures to prove it to the rest of us. Pick your favorite social media feed. Scroll for ninety seconds. You'll probably find someone with before-and-after pictures, saying something like, "I don't normally post selfies, but I want everyone to know about how much happier I feel now that I'm on the Keto-Whole-Thirty-Daniel-Fast-Eat-Like-A-Neanderthal diet." All your friends are either quitting something or starting something and inviting us to follow along their self-guided journey to a stronger, braver, and sexier *me*.

---

[6] Lewis, *Mere Christianity*, 11.

The idea that you can change yourself is just as ancient as the idea that you shouldn't change at all. The whole self-help movement is just a watered-down version of a Christian heresy called *Pelagianism.* Named for Pelagius, the thought leader behind the philosophy, it advocated the idea that we could change our habits if we would just try harder. According to his thinking, there is nothing inherently unfixable about us. We can be as brave, as strong, as sexy, *as perfect* as we set out to be. Just set your mind to it. Sign up for a few more memberships. Watch our ten-minute introductory video, and we'll have you fixed up in no time (for a small monthly payment of $19.95).

Even if we do manage to change our habits on our own, many of us still fear that there is something unchanged within us. Whatever changes we make feel surface-level and short-term at best. Despite all the external progress we've made, it still feels like there is something internal resisting all these positive changes. We end up living in a kind of restless paranoia, haunted by the possibility that the habits we hate will sneak up on us again. We're afraid that our stories, like many of the stories featured in *Hoarders* or *Biggest Loser,* will end with a paragraph saying something like, "Six months after we recorded this episode, he had fallen back into his old habits again." The weight is back, the lying has started again, the pornography found another way into my life, Saturday morning headaches are the norm again, and I'm sleeping with someone I met on Tinder last night. Despite what our social media feeds are saying, we're living in constant fear of being found out.

The God Who Changes Us

Many young adults live in the tension of feeling like we should change but also feeling like we can't change. In the song "Happy to Be Here," twenty-something songwriter Julien Baker captures what it feels like to inhabit this tension:

> If I could do what I want I'd become an electrician
>
> I'd climb inside my ears and I'd rearrange the wires in my brain
>
> A different me would be inhabiting this body
>
> Have two cars, a garage, a job, and would go to church on Sunday

It feels like there is some "faulty circuitry" up there, but she isn't sure what to do about it. Even though we live in an age where we can fix anything, she finds herself asking, "Then why, then why, then why, then why not me?" Finally, she lands where many of us land after struggling to change, singing, "I know I should be optimistic but I'm doubtful I can change." Like many young adults, she's living somewhere between optimism and doubt, hope and cynicism—struggling to make sense of her life.

Or consider Cheryl Strayed, the author of *Wild*—a memoir about hiking the Pacific Crest Trail as a twenty-something. She moved to Portland, hoping to escape her old life and start over, only to find that her problems followed her. Addicted to heroin, she felt the inward tug-of-war, writing,

> In the bathroom, I'd wash my face and sob into my hands for a few fast breaths, getting ready for the waitressing job I'd picked up at a breakfast place. I'd think: *This is not me. This is not the way I am. Stop it. No more.* But in the afternoons I'd return with a wad of cash to buy another bit of heroin and I'd think: *Yes. I get to do this. I get to waste my life. I get to be junk.*[7]

As much as she wanted to change, she continually fell back into her addiction. Wanting to change wasn't enough to change her.

Near the middle of a lengthy letter to a church in Rome, Saint Paul spirals into the heart of what Augustine, Julien Baker, and Cheryl Strayed later echo, saying, "For I have the desire to do what it is right, but not the ability to carry it out. For I do not do the good that I want, but the evil that I do not want is what I keep on doing" (Rom. 7:18–19). He's restless just like the rest of us. *I was ravished into your presence by your beauty, but soon torn away from you by the weight of myself,* writes Augustine. *I know I should be optimistic but I'm doubtful I can change,* sings Julien Baker. *This is not me. This is not the way I am. Stop it. No more,* writes Cheryl Strayed. We want to change, but we feel like we can't.

There is something more going on within us than neuroscience can explain, something outside of the bounds of the scientific method. Returning to the concept of chunking, it seems like there is already something hardwired into us, something beyond our

---

[7] Cheryl Strayed, *Wild: From Lost to Found on the Pacific Crest Trail* (New York: Vintage Books, 2013), 53.

control, that makes our brains more likely to chunk the habits we hate. Something is greasing the pathways into the habits that are destroying us, making it easy for us to slide into them and nearly impossible to climb out of them.

In *Unapologetic*, Francis Spufford calls this force the human propensity to mess things up no matter how hard we try to do otherwise—using slightly edgier and angrier language than I've paraphrased here.[8] Trying to understand this force or propensity for himself, Saint Paul continues the earlier thought, saying,

> Now if I do what I do not want, it is no longer I who do it, but sin that dwells within me. So I find it to be a law that when I want to do right, evil lies close at hand. For I delight in the law of God, in my inner being, but I see in my members another law waging war against the law of my mind and making me captive to the law of sin that dwells in my members. (Rom. 7:20–23)

Sin is more than something you do wrong or a habit you form. It's a power, a force, a propensity at work within you from the moment you were born. It's resisting even your smallest steps in a positive direction. It makes you want what you don't want, crave what you don't crave, and love the habits you hate. As long as this fact remains unchanged, you will never find rest in trying to change or in staying the same.

---

[8] Francis Spufford, *Unapologetic: Why, Despite Everything, Christianity Can Still Make Surprising Emotional Sense* (New York: HarperOne, 2013), 27.

It's here, at the end of ourselves, tiptoeing on the edge of resigned cynicism about the possibility of change, shaking our fists and yelling at the sky, that we feel something akin to what Paul feels at the end of this passage. He writes, speaking of his own firsthand experience of our shared dilemma, "Wretched man that I am! Who will save me from this body of death?" (Rom. 7:24). It's from this place of desperation, when we're on our knees screaming for help to anyone in the uncaring universe who might be listening, that we're finally in a place where we can find rest in the God who changes us.

Paul's question precedes one of the greatest turns in all of Scripture. In the next verse, Paul answers his own question, saying, "Thanks be to God through Jesus Christ our Lord" (Rom. 7:25). In the life, death, and resurrection of Jesus Christ, God has done something about our condition. He has seen us in our distress, stuck like flies in a glue trap (to steal a metaphor from Augustine), and entered right into the midst of it.

We will never find rest in trying to change ourselves or in refusing to change ourselves, but only in the God who has arrived to change what we cannot. It's why twelve-step programs tend to start with realizing that we cannot change ourselves and trusting in a power greater than ourselves to do something about it. God has done what Paul, what *we*, cannot do. It's not because we deserve it or because he wanted to meet us halfway, but out of the overflow of his love for us. True change begins here, not with something we do, but with trusting in something God has already done.

Tim Chester, in his book *You Can Change*, writes, "Sin arises because we desire something more than we desire God. Overcoming sin begins by reversing this process: desiring God more than other things."[9] We can't re-orient this habit-forming desire on our own, but as Paul writes at the beginning of the next chapter, God can. Paul writes, "The law of the Spirit of life has set you free in Christ Jesus from the law of sin and death" (Rom. 8:2). Through his Holy Spirit, God kicks free the stuck rudder of desire and reorients it toward himself. The only way we can desire God more than other things is if God steps in and does something about it. That's grace.

Near the end of Book Eight of *Confessions*, amid the inward struggle between wanting and not wanting, Augustine runs out into the garden behind where he was staying and throws himself to the ground. Then, seemingly out of nowhere, he starts to hear the voice of what sounds like a little child, saying, "Pick it up! Read it! Pick it up! Read it!" Uncertain of what to do with this voice, he picks up a Bible and reads the first verse he comes across. It ends up being Romans 13:13–14, which says, "Let us behave decently, as in the daytime, not in carousing and drunkenness, not in sexual immorality and debauchery, not in dissension and jealousy. Rather, clothe yourselves with the Lord Jesus Christ, and do not think about how to gratify the desires of the flesh."

After reading this passage, Augustine says, "The instant I finished this sentence, my heart was

---

[9] Tim Chester, *You Can Change: God's Transforming Power for Our Sinful Behavior and Negative Emotions* (Wheaton: Crossway, 2010), 106.

virtually flooded with a light of relief and certitude, and all the darkness of my hesitation scattered away" (8.29). In that moment, the final domino in a long series, God turned Augustine toward himself, changing what Augustine could not change. It was from that moment onward that Augustine could say, "With your right hand, you explored the depths of my death, and from the floor of my heart you drained out the sea of rot. But the whole of what brought this about was that I stopped wanting what *I* had been wanting, and instead wanted what *you* wanted" (9.1). Struggle remained for the rest of his life, but sin was no longer a tyrant.

When God sets us free from the power of sin, the habits that once felt irresistible can be resisted. The possibility of forgiveness instead of anger suddenly seems imaginable. The urge to click the link that will wreck your night loses its urgency. The tendency to take instead of give begins to lose some of its momentum. The habit loops are still there, but they have been irreversibly weakened. We are still living in the aftermath of years of untamed habits, but something about us has been fundamentally changed.

While the habits themselves do not change automatically, it's from this place that we can begin to change the habits we hate, what Paul calls the "deeds of the body" (Rom. 8:13). Instead of changing from a place of restlessness, we get to change from a place of rest. Instead of changing from a place of fear, we get to change from a place of freedom. Instead of changing to avoid condemnation, we get to change from a pronouncement of *no condemnation* over us. Change will still require work, but it's a kind of work free from the crushing anxiety normally associated with change. From this new craving, this new desire, this new love, we can start to form the habits God loves, which we will soon discover are the habits we were made for.

As long as we live in our earthly bodies, we will still experience resistance to change, but thanks be to God we are no longer helpless against it. While the habits we hate are no longer inevitable, it's easy to get frustrated, depressed, and angry when we continue to struggle with something—even if we are on the winning side. Unless we have hope for something beyond this world, it's easy to spiral back into our former restlessness. Paul, speaking to those of us who might be losing hope, writes this: "We ourselves, who have the firstfruits of the Spirit, groan inwardly as we wait eagerly for adoption as sons, the redemption of our bodies" (Rom. 8:23). A day is coming when "we shall all be changed, in a moment, in the twinkling of an eye" (1 Cor. 15:51–52), and we will be made into someone completely new. We can rest not only in the fact that we *have been* changed but also that one day we *will be* changed.

3

SEARCHING FOR BELONGING

Yet, I couldn't be happy without friends—not even according to my understanding of happiness at the time—no matter how sumptuous my physical pleasures might be.

– Augustine, *Confessions* (6.26)

This scares me. More than finding the right job or city or spouse—I'm scared of losing this web we're in. This elusive, indefinable, opposite of loneliness. This feeling I feel right now.

– Marina Keegan, age 22

When I was eight years old, I was kicked out of the Cherry Hill Drive Beanie Baby Club. *I'm not crying, you're crying.*

Beanie Babies were the fidget spinners of '97. They were little plush animals full of beans that you could buy in the variety stores located in the dimly lit corners of strip malls. Each animal had a heart-shaped tag with a date of birth and a cute little poem on the inside. According to our price guides, they were destined to be worth hundreds of dollars in the not-so-distant future. And, for some inexplicable reason, everyone my age wanted them.

In honor of the fad, the elementary schoolers of Beaverton's Cherry Hill Drive decided to form an exclusive society in which we could talk about and trade Beanie Babies. There were five of us: Brian, J.J., Shawn, Hannah, and myself. As the resident third-graders, Hannah and J.J. were the assumed leaders.

I was late to the first meeting. I brought Tuffy, a brown terrier and my only Beanie Baby at the time. I had not given much thought to the fact that everyone else had more than one animal until one of the leaders spoke up on behalf of the whole club and said something like, "Austin, we're sorry to inform you that you are required to have more than one Beanie Baby in order to be part of the club." I had failed to read the bylaws. With that, I was kicked out of the Cherry Hill Drive Beanie Baby Club, never to return.

As I walked in the front door, weeping with the tears characteristic of sensitive children like myself, my dad asked me what was wrong. I responded with a sentence my dad is still quoting twenty years later, saying, "I was excluded from the Beanie Baby Club!" I'm not sure when or where I learned the word *excluded*, but I knew it described what I had just experienced at the Beanie Baby Club.

While trying to conceal his laughter, my dad comforted me by offering to help me form my own club. He helped me create my own website, complete with Beanie Baby GIFs and downloadable bylaws for my own club (of which I was the president). In the bylaws, I made only one rule: *anyone can be part of the club no matter how many Beanie Babies you have.* No one joined my club, and the Cherry Hill Drive Beanie Baby Club disbanded due to lack of interest and attention spans.

Everyone has a childhood memory of wondering where they belong. It might have been an experience of not getting a part in *Footloose* or not making the little league team. It might have been moving to a new city and starting at a new school without any friends. It might have been that moment when everyone was talking about seeing *Titanic* but your parents didn't allow you to see it so you had to pretend you did. Brené Brown, after recounting her own experience of being left out in *Braving the Wilderness*, writes, "These are the moments that when left unspoken and unresolved, send us into our adult lives searching desperately for belonging and settling for fitting in."[1] We crave belonging, but for so many of us, the search is amplified by a dozen experiences of feeling left out.

The *clubs* might change a bit as we age, but the search for belonging nags us throughout young adulthood. We are transitioning out of secure and stable relationships, built through two decades' worth of conversations, and into less stable environments like a new college or a new city. We're trying to find friends, trying to find a community to call our own, trying to find people who can be something like family. In our cultural moment, some of us over-belong to tribes, others of us live with the under-belonging of loneliness, and most of us inhabit the uneasy tension somewhere between the two.

In "The Opposite of Loneliness," an essay written just before her tragic death at 22, Marina Keegan describes the encroaching feeling of loneliness that

---

[1] Brené Brown, *Braving the Wilderness: The Quest for True Belonging and the Courage to Stand Alone* (New York: Random House, 2017), 13.

sneaks up when you are about to transition out of college and into something else. In the opening few paragraphs, she writes about her experience at Yale:

> We don't have a word for the opposite of loneliness, but if we did, I could say that's what I want in life. What I'm grateful and thankful to have found at Yale, and what I'm scared of losing when we wake up tomorrow and leave this place.
>
> It's not quite love and it's not quite community; it's just this feeling that there are people, an abundance of people, who are in this together. Who are on your team. When the check is paid and you stay at the table. When it's four a.m. and no one goes to bed. That night with the guitar. That night we can't remember. That time we did, we went, we saw, we laughed, we felt. The hats.
>
> Yale is full of tiny circles we pull around ourselves. A cappella groups, sports teams, houses, societies, clubs. These tiny groups that make us feel loved and safe and part of something even on our loneliest nights when we stumble home to our computers—partner-less, tired, awake. We won't have those next year. We won't live on the same block as all our friends. We won't have a bunch of group-texts.
>
> This scares me. More than finding the right job or city or spouse—I'm scared of losing this web

we're in. This elusive, indefinable, opposite of loneliness. This feeling I feel right now.[2]

I have found nothing that better captures what young adults feel about belonging. We want the opposite of loneliness. We want to belong to something, to *someone*. We know that we cannot live without it. No one wants to live as a half.

I Didn't Want to Live as a Half

Augustine longed to be liked. He was a classic case of a teenager who ignored every high school P.S.A. about not giving in to peer pressure. He was not *Above the Influence*. He couldn't *Just Say No*. As one who "yearned for approval in human eyes" (2.1), he would have jumped off the bridge if all his friends were doing it. When his classmates told locker room stories of terrible crimes they had done, ashamed of his own innocence, he pretended that he had also done the same (2.7).

Faking it became reality when his friends invited him to steal from a neighborhood pear tree. He never would have done it alone, he says, but he "loved the company" of those with whom he committed the crime (2.16). His terrible, adolescent choices were less about a craving for a certain illicit activity and more about his craving to belong. The habits he grew to hate in his twenties started with a longing to be liked in his teens. He cared too much about what his friends thought to think for himself. His teenage

---

[2] Marina Keegan, "The Opposite of Loneliness," *The Opposite of Loneliness: Essays and Stories* (New York: Scribner, 2014), 1.

squad was, in his own words, a "friendship that couldn't be more unfriendly" (2.17). They were the friends you invite to your wedding and hope no one gives them a microphone.

Moving on from his *bro*-mob, Augustine developed one particularly close bond. It was an "excessively sweet friendship, cooked up in the heat of similar pursuits" (4.7). It was with this friend that Augustine experienced the kind of deep friendship that C.S. Lewis would later describe as opening with "What? You too? I thought I was the only one."[3] It lasted just over a year before ending tragically.

In an essay from the early '80s, David Foster Wallace described what depression feels like from the inside.[4] Everyone knows the "less than fun" feeling of what it's like to be sick to your stomach, he says, but imagine "your whole body being sick like that" and you're close to knowing what it's like to suffer from depression. Everything falls apart from the inside, and no one can see it happening except you. It's why Wallace would later describe it as "the invisible torment" in *Infinite Jest*.[5]

When Augustine's closest friend died suddenly, he collapsed into Wallace's invisible torment. "Only weeping was pleasant to me," he writes (4.9). The experience sent him into an introspective tailspin. He writes, "I was wretched, and every mind is wretched when it is chained to friendship with things bound to

---

[3] C.S. Lewis, *The Four Loves* (New York: Harcourt, 1988), 65.

[4] David Foster Wallace, "The Planet Trillaphon as it Stands in Relation to a Bad Thing," in *The David Foster Wallace Reader* (New York: Hatchette, 2014), 5–19.

[5] David Foster Wallace, *Infinite Jest* (New York, NY: Back Bay Books, 2016), 697.

die, and is torn to shreds when it loses them" (4.11). The loneliness of loss left him wondering if friendship was even worth it, if he was willing to risk knowing and being known only to watch it all evaporate. He poured his life into that friendship, saying, "I felt that my soul and the soul of the other had been a single one in two bodies, and for that reason life was pure horror to me, because I didn't want to live as a half" (4.11). It is often not until the funeral of a friend, one initiated by physical death or even by moving to another city, that you realize how attached you were. *I didn't want to live as a half* is more familiar than we admit.

Augustine, still hoping that belonging would solve his problems, threw himself entirely into his friendships with equal—if not greater—intensity. He remained with the Manicheans longer than he believed their teachings because he had "more intimate friendships with the Manicheans" than he had "with people outside this heretical sect" (5.19). To walk away from his sense of belonging was to risk what Brené Brown calls *the wilderness*, "an untamed, unpredictable place of solitude and searching."[6] There is an emotional safety, a certainty amidst an uncertain life, that comes with being in community with others. Augustine would rather have lived a lie with friends than live alone in truth.

In his twenties, Augustine lived with two friends, Nebridius and Alypius. He eventually left the Manicheans as the three of them lived together in the "blazing pursuit of truth and wisdom" (6.17). They

---

[6] Brown, *Braving the Wilderness*, 36.

stayed up late solving philosophical dilemmas about death and the meaning of life. They urged one another to never get married so they could be free to pursue wisdom without any other concerns (this was obviously a pre-video games era). At one point, Augustine even crafted plans to form a kind of fraternity, saying,

> We despised the uproarious annoyances of human life and were on the brink of resolving to live in retired leisure away from the mob. We were going to engineer this leisure by placing everything we could lay our hands on into a joint holding and thus create a single combined household estate. In the integrity of friendship, we would see that things didn't belong to us individually, but instead, what came from the entire community would be unified, and this would belong to each of us, and each item to everyone. (6.24)

Two of them would work to cover expenses each year while the rest of them were free to converse, read, and write. The whole plan crumbled when Augustine realized that the spouses of those already married were not on board for living in a commune.

Augustine's life revolved around his friendships. When one tribe couldn't do it for him any more, he found another tribe that could. When he lost one friend to death, he found two more friends to make up for it. If there was one thing Augustine could not live without, it was a sense of belonging: "I couldn't be happy without friends" (6.26).

When Your Friends Get Married,
the Fun Gets Buried

I had attempted something like Augustine's fraternity in college. It was not a fraternity in the Greek-letters sense, but we did live in a kind of brotherhood with one another. At my end of the dorm, there were a few of us who began to share in the same daily rhythms. One person was in charge of waking the rest of us at the same time every day and getting the French press ready. We would spend the morning reading and conversing over coffee while everyone else slept. For the thirty minutes before breakfast, we would divide up and find some solitude. After solitude, we would meet for breakfast in the mostly empty cafeteria.

Unlike most students, we stayed on campus during the weekends. Some of us stayed because home was far away and others because campus had become home. One weekend, we invented Cart-a-Pult, which involved one of us getting into a shopping cart, three others pushing it into a snow pile, and someone else marking our flight distance. Another weekend, we spent three hours piling leaves outside my second-floor window, and the next two hours jumping out my window into the pile. With friends who lived only a few feet away, a sense of belonging came easily. It was the opposite of loneliness.

When I moved back home after college, hundreds of miles away from my college friends, it was just me and my wife. I was in my hometown, but I had burned my bridges when I moved away four years earlier, purging Facebook of all but a few of my high-school friendships, planning never to live there again. *Adults aren't supposed to feel lonely*, I thought, *so why do I?* I had no inside jokes with anyone. My wife and I had just gotten married, yet I still felt like I was living as a half.

Loneliness is notoriously difficult to explain. It's not the same as being alone, nor is it magically healed by surrounding yourself with other warm bodies. It's what you feel when you're not sure who you can trust when things go wrong. It's what you feel when someone asks you who your best friend is and you're not sure how to answer. It's what you feel when you haven't opened up in months to anyone about what's really going on in your life; you have an extra ticket to something and you're not sure who to invite; you're not sure where to go for Thanksgiving; Facebook is the only reason anyone knows it's your birthday; no one volunteers to pick you up at the airport. It's what you feel when you've been excluded from the Beanie Baby Club.

In *The Lonely City*, Olivia Laing wrote about her own experience with urban loneliness, pairing her plight with that of different artists throughout the twentieth century. Trying to describe what loneliness feels like from the inside, she writes,

> What does it feel like to be lonely? It feels like being hungry when everyone around you is readying for a feast. It feels shameful and alarming, and over time these feelings radiate outwards, making the lonely person increasingly isolated, increasingly estranged. It hurts, in the way that feelings do, and it also has physical consequences that take place invisibly, inside the closed compartments of the body. It advances, is

what I'm trying to say, as cold as ice and clear
as glass, enclosing and engulfing.[7]

In another chapter, Laing continues the analogy of
loneliness as feeling like you are trapped in a block of
ice. You can see everyone else, but for some reason
you can't make contact with them (or at least not as
much contact as you would like).[8] When magician David Blaine encased himself in ice for sixty-three hours
in 2000, he said that he would never attempt a stunt
of that difficulty again. For the lonely, it seems, that's
just everyday life.

According to a 2018 study, as many as 50 percent
of Americans feel left out or alone sometimes or always.[9] Half of us feel like we are living as a half, and
young adults are the loneliest of all. On the UCLA
Loneliness Scale, which uses twenty questions to as-
sess how thick your block of ice is, Millennials and
members of Generation Z scored the highest. It's safe
to assume that every other person you meet is lonely.

Young adulthood is a nonstop series of friendship
funerals. You have a funeral when you graduate high
school. Then, you have another one when you graduate college. It's followed quickly by a series of friends
who get married and another series of cross-country
moves by friends who are taking jobs. They are funerals without hearses or homilies or little orange flags
on a procession of cars—just you, mourning a loss no

---

[7] Olivia Laing, *The Lonely City: Adventures in the Art of Being
Alone* (New York: Picador, 2016), 12.

[8] Laing, *The Lonely City*, 26.

[9] "New Cigna Study Reveals Loneliness at Epidemic Levels in
America," May 1, 2018, https://www.multivu.com/players/Eng-
lish/8294451–cigna-us-loneliness-survey.

one else feels. Regular dinners turn into trying to find space in the calendar three months from now. Late-night conversations turn into texting one another *we should chat soon,* only to never follow up. As my brother once wrote in a song, "When your friends get married, the fun gets buried." If your twenties were on a chart, the friendship arrow is moving steadily downward as your age continues to move upward.

The rise in loneliness among young adults has only been magnified by the ubiquity of digital devices. Sherry Turkle, MIT professor and author of *Alone To-gether* and *Reclaiming Conversation,* argues that social media is only giving us the illusion of belonging while actually adding to our sense of feeling alone. She writes, "Digital connections . . . may offer the il-lusion of companionship without the demands of friendship. Our networked life allows us to hide from each other, even as we are tethered to each other. We'd rather text than talk."[10] For those of us who have grown up never knowing a world without digital tech-nology, this tech-induced loneliness is the new normal.

The new normal has inspired initiatives like *The Loneliness Project,* which is dedicated to telling real stories of loneliness submitted by people.[11] It's led to the appointment of a Minister of Loneliness in the United Kingdom.[12] In Blackpool, England, a non-

---

[10] Sherry Turkle, *Alone Together: Why We Expect More from Technology and Less from Each Other* (New York: Basic Books, 2011), 1.

[11] See www.thelonelinessproject.org.

[12] Ceylan Yeginsu, "U.K. Appoints a Loneliness Minister," *The New York Times,* online, January 17, 2018,

profit organization opened a public space called The Living Room where people can stay all day and spend time with other humans.[13] We're trying to find ways to cope with our loneliness, the perpetual sense of under-belonging, and as a result we're in danger of falling into the other extreme.

Welcome to Thumbsuckers Anonymous

In the same year I was excluded from the Beanie Baby Club, I discovered the power of belonging to a tribe of like-minded friends at school. My second-grade teacher, Mrs. Bunch, had asked our class if any of us could name a good habit. As someone who loved to talk, regardless of whether I had anything to say, I raised my hand and said, "I don't know what a good habit is, but I know a bad one: *sucking my thumb.*" I told the class about my struggle to quit sucking my thumb and how my parents had unsuccessfully tried to break me by rubbing hot sauce into my thumb, coating my thumbnail with an invisible polish that tasted like living death, and asking me to wear socks on my hands for entire evenings. Two other students, Molly and Jarod, admitted to sharing the same struggle. Seeing an opportunity, Mrs. Bunch formed a discussion group with the three of us: Thumbsuckers Anonymous. I kept up my addiction for two more years, but at least I had company.

---

https://www.nytimes.com/2018/01/17/world/europe/uk-brit-ain-loneliness.html.

[13] Jessica Leigh Hester, "Fighting Loneliness with Public Living Rooms," *CityLab*, November 4, 2016, http://www.citylab.com/navigator/2016/11/fighting-loneliness-with-public-living-rooms/506360.

It feels good to belong to a tribe, to know that you're not alone. A sense of belonging releases brain chemicals that literally make us feel good.[14] We were made for life together. In an era dominated by what *The New York Times* columnist David Brooks calls "flock comedies"—shows that revolve around a group of tight-knit friends—many young adults expect to quickly find a tribe to call their own.[15] "With people delaying marriage and childbearing into their 30s," writes Brooks, "young people now spend long periods of their lives outside of traditional families, living among diverse friendship tribes." Augustine had Alypius and Nebridius; Ross has Joey and Chandler. We want to belong to a tribe of people whose apartments we can walk into without knocking, whose cereal we can eat without asking, and whose couches we can crash on when we're too tired to go home.

In addition to friendship tribes, the Internet has made it easier to surround ourselves with tribes of people who share our religious beliefs, our cultural preferences, and our political leanings. In cities full of people different than us, we're finding ways to live among people just like us. In a TED Talk from 2009, Seth Godin explains the rise of tribes:

> Lots of people are used to having a spiritual tribe, or a church tribe, having a work tribe, having a community tribe. But now, thanks to the Internet, thanks to the explosion of mass media,

---

[14] Simon Sinek, *Leaders Eat Last: Why Some Teams Pull Together and Others Don't* (New York: Penguin, 2017), 57–62.

[15] David Brooks, "The Flock Comedies," *The New York Times*, online, October 21, 2010, https://www.nytimes.com/2010/10/22/opinion/22brooks.html?_r=3&hp.

thanks to a lot of other things that are bubbling up through our society around the world, tribes are everywhere.

The Internet was supposed to homogenize everyone by connecting us all. Instead what it's allowed is silos of interest. So you've got the red-hat ladies over here. You've got the red-hat tri-athletes over there. You've got the organized armies over here. You've got the disorganized rebels over here. You've got people in white hats making food. And people in white hats sailing boats. The point is that you can find Ukrainian folk dancers and connect with them, because you want to be connected. That people on the fringes can find each other, connect and go somewhere.[16]

In my own city, I've found a tribe of Scrabble players, a tribe of ultimate Frisbee players, and a tribe of young adults who want to make a difference. Thanks to websites like Meetup, in a few clicks you can find a tribe you didn't know existed five minutes earlier.

Our innate desire for belonging is leading us toward a dangerous over-belonging. It's a sense of belonging in which we set our tribe against other tribes and develop an us-versus-them mentality about everything. We develop an insider language that makes any attempt at conversation with outsiders dead on arrival. We read only articles written by people who reinforce our opinions, follow only the

---

[16] Seth Godin, "The Tribes We Lead," filmed February 2009 at TED2009, https://www.ted.com/talks/seth_godin_on_the_tribes_we_lead/transcript?language=en.

celebrities who say things we like, and hang out only with people who complain how we complain and celebrate what we celebrate.

Journalist Bill Bishop documents the phenomenon of over-belonging in his book *The Big Sort*. Not only are we using the Internet to find our tribes, we're more and more geographically buffered from people who think differently. Just look at the concentrations of red and blue on an election map. The effect is a loss of empathy and ability to listen to anyone different, and it's making all of us more extreme. He writes, "Mixed company moderates; like-minded company polarizes. Heterogeneous communities retain group excesses; homogenous communities march toward the extremes."[17] Opposite the view that pins religion as the instigator of extremism, this kind of attitude is only becoming more common as people become less and less religious.[18]

We end up believing, saying, and doing things we would never do on our own. As in Augustine's teenage experience in Carthage, we end up with friendships that couldn't be more unfriendly. We end up in communities like the Manicheans that exert manipulative pressure on you if you think differently. And, even when we belong to a tribe, it's still hard to shake the sense that we don't actually belong.

Meg Jay says, "Most twenty-somethings yearn for a feeling of community, and they cling to their strong

---

[17] Bill Bishop, *The Big Sort: Why the Clustering of Like-Minded America is Tearing Us Apart* (New York: Mariner Books, 2009), 68.

[18] Peter Beinart, "Breaking Faith," *The Atlantic,* online, April 2017, https://www.theatlantic.com/magazine/archive/2017/04/breaking-faith/517785.

ties to feel more connected. Ironically, being en-
meshed with a group can actually enhance feelings of
isolation, because we—and our tribe—become insular
and detached."[19] Brené Brown, in her book on belonging, notices the same trend. Why are both loneliness
and tribalism, under-belonging and over-belonging,
on the rise? She concludes, "Clearly, selecting like-
minded friends and neighbors and separating ourselves as much as possible from people whom we
think of as different from us has not delivered the
deep sense of belonging that we are hardwired to
crave."[20] Modern tribalism has not rescued us from
the intense loneliness so many of us are running
from. We still long to belong.

Are You All Some Kind of Family?

In *Braving the Wilderness*, Brown explains the complexities of the search for belonging in our cultural
moment. Her answer to these twin problems of tribalism and loneliness is a "theory of true belonging," a
sense of belonging that frees you from the pain of
loneliness and the dangers of tribalism.[21] She writes,
"True belonging is not something that you negotiate
externally, it's what you carry in your heart."[22] *True
belonging*, according to Brown, sounds very much like
the *rest* Augustine speaks about. It's belonging that
allows you to be alone without being lonely and with
others without living for their approval. It's not fragile,
dependent on the quality of your current web of

---

[19] Jay, *The Defining Decade*, 27.
[20] Brown, *Braving the Wilderness*, 51.
[21] Ibid., 28.
[22] Ibid., 40.

relationships. Instead of looking *for* belonging, you're free to enjoy community or solitude as one who is living *from* belonging.

But where do you find true belonging? For Brown, it's found in "believing in and belonging to yourself."[23] In other words, according to her, the rest you're looking for is found by looking inward rather than outward. It's found in developing a strong sense of who you are and having the courage to be who you are no matter who you're with.

While I can affirm that true belonging is not something you negotiate externally with others, I cannot affirm that it's something you negotiate internally with yourself. A sense of belonging dependent on what you think of yourself is no less fragile than one dependent on what others think of you. Whatever true belonging is, wherever rest is to be found, we must look further than ourselves.

In the Gospel of Mark, one of four accounts in the Bible about the life of Jesus, there is a scene in which we see a sense of belonging that's free from both us-versus-them tribalism and paralyzing loneliness. A young man had just walked away crushed after a conversation with Jesus. The young man had asked about the secret to eternal life and, in response, Jesus invited him to join his fledgling community. But first there was a move to make: "You lack one thing," Jesus told him: "Go, sell all that you have and give to the poor, and you will have treasure in heaven; and come follow me" (Mark 10:21). It was too much to ask.

---

[23] Ibid., 40.

After the man walked away, Jesus and Peter (one of his earliest followers) had the following conversation about what there is to gain from following him:

> Peter began to say to him, "See, we have left everything and followed you."

> Jesus said, "Truly, I say to you, there is no one who has left house or brothers or sisters or mother or father or children or lands, for my sake and for the gospel, who will not receive a hundredfold now in this time, houses and brothers and sisters and mothers and children and lands, with persecutions, and in the age to come eternal life. But many who are first will be last, and the last first." (Mark 10:28–31)

Jesus speaks of a family, a sense of belonging, that is one hundred times better than anything you've ever known. There is something to be found in Jesus, something you can carry with you, that frees you to leave your tribe, your loneliness, or both.

First, we're less tribal because of what we leave behind. In Mark 10:28, Peter told Jesus that they left everything to follow him: careers, hometowns, and families. In the first century, the family was the primary form of belonging.[24] Even though your family was your tribe, Jesus called his followers to be part of something else. For example, consider how James and John responded to Jesus: "And going on a little farther, he saw James the son of Zebedee and John his brother, who were in their boat mending the nets.

---

[24] See Chapter 3 of Joseph H. Hellerman, *When the Church Was a Family* (Nashville: B&H Academic, 2009).

And immediately he called them, and *they left their father Zebedee* in the boat with the hired servants and followed him" (Mark 1:19–20).

Leaving our primary forms of belonging, whether it's people who share the same last name or friends we've known since college, is part of what it means to follow Jesus. In one case, he used some strong language to make his point, saying, "If anyone comes to me and does not *hate* his own father and mother and wife and children and brothers and sisters, yes, and even his own life, he cannot be my disciple" (Luke 14:26–27). Jesus is not using the word *hate* like we use the word. As a Semitic idiom, *hate* means something like "cast aside" or "abandon" one's tribe, or even yourself, as your primary allegiance or loyalty.[25]

By leaving their group loyalties, they were able to join with people from other cultural tribes. In Mark 3:13–19, when we get a glimpse into the core group of followers Jesus chose, we see that it included people from different ends of the political spectrum: a tax collector who sold his soul to the empire and a political zealot who sold his soul to bringing it down. It's what we see in *The Fellowship of the Ring* when elves, dwarves, men, hobbits, and a wizard come together to destroy the ring of power. In both cases, individuals were required to *hate* old loyalties and cling to new ones.

If the church is considered a tribe, it's meant to be the tribe where *tribalism* goes to die—a reality it often gets wrong. It's where we leave behind any sense of belonging based on politics, ethnicity, biology, or

---

[25] Hellerman, *When the Church Was a Family*, 68.

affinity. My dad, looking out at the congregation on a Sunday morning, has often said, "Where else in the world would you find *this* group of people?" Our churches should not make sense according to our cultural standards of belonging.

Second, we're less lonely because of what we gain in place of what we've left behind. When we leave our old forms of belonging, even if it feels as if we had nothing to leave, we gain a new family in place of the old one. In *When the Church Was a Family*, Joseph Hellerman writes, "Again, exchanging one family for another is at the heart of what it means to be a disciple of Jesus."[26] Jesus was not "family-friendly" in either the first-century or modern-day sense of the phrase. He did not say, "Seek first your family and everything else will be added unto you." Instead, he reimagined what it meant to be family.

Instead of defining family according to biology, Jesus defines family as those who are committed to reordering their lives around who God is, what God has done, and what God has said. In Mark 3:31–35, we see how Jesus interacts with his own biological family:

> And his mother and his brothers came, and standing outside they sent to him and called him. And a crowd was sitting around him, and they said to him, "Your mother and your brothers are outside, seeking you." And he answered them, "Who are my mother and my brothers?" And looking about at those who sat around him, he said, "Here are my mother and my brothers!

[26] Ibid., 68.

For whoever does the will of God, he is my brother and sister and mother."

It's why Paul, who wrote many of the letters in the New Testament, uses family language to talk about the church. He uses *brother* and *sister* to talk about other believers. It's why my friends from more charismatic churches call me "Brother Austin," a constant reminder of who my true family is.

For singles, couples who can't have kids, those who live far away from their relatives, or anyone who might be lonely, Jesus' vision of family is good news. In my first year as a pastor, I asked a new person about his family, and he responded by saying, "I don't have a family." He never knew his biological mom or dad, and he had been in and out of foster homes for his entire life. Without even thinking, I responded, "If you want, we can be your family." Not long after that conversation, we were all cooking out in the park and someone asked us, "Are all of you some kind of family?" My wife was the first to respond: "Yes, something like that."

When I was growing up, my parents chose to open up our home to a woman from our church who did not have any biological family nearby. I would come home from school and she would be in our house. She came to our birthday parties, took us on adventures in downtown Portland, came over for dinner whenever she felt like it, and even attended grandparents' day festivities at my elementary school. Thanks to the way my parents practiced the art of including others in our family, I had a difficult time distinguishing who was part of our family and who was not.

When we follow Jesus, we leave behind our tribes and join a new family. True belonging, though, is still not found *in* this new family—even if it might be found *through* it. Dietrich Bonhoeffer, writing to German believers in the midst of the Third Reich, says,

> Many people seek fellowship because they are afraid to be alone. Because they cannot stand loneliness, they are driven to seek the company of other people. There are Christians, too, who cannot endure being alone, who have had some bad experiences with themselves, who hope they will gain some help in association with others. They are generally disappointed. Then they blame the fellowship for what is really their own fault. The Christian community is not a spiritual sanatorium. The person who comes into a fellowship because he is running away from himself is misusing it for the sake of diversion, no matter how spiritual this diversion may appear.[27]

When we try to find belonging in others, even in other believers, we're in danger of depending on others to be more than what they can be. We still need a sense of belonging that is not externally or internally negotiated, something that can survive even when others are not there.

After Augustine lost his best friend, he reflected on where true belonging, *true rest*, can be found. It cannot be found in friends, even Christian friends, he suggests. Instead, he writes, "it's a happy person who loves *you*, God, and in you loves his friend, and loves

---

[27] Dietrich Bonhoeffer, *Life Together: The Classic Exploration of Christian Community* (New York: HarperOne, 1954), 76.

his enemy because of you. The only one who never loses anyone dear to him is the one to whom everyone is dear through him who can't be lost" (4.14). According to Augustine, true belonging can be found only when one's whole life is directed toward God. From this place, you can belong to those you would consider friends and even to those who by every measure should be considered enemies. It doesn't mean you'll never be lonely, but it does mean that your loneliness no longer has to define you. It's resting in God that frees you into a different kind of belonging, one that is not dependent on others or yourself, but on the One who does not change, who does not leave, who does not die. This is true belonging, the opposite of loneliness.

SEARCHING FOR LOVE

I wasn't in love yet, but I was in love with the prospect of being in love.

— Augustine, *Confessions* (3.1)

I don't need a piece of paper to prove my love to someone. That's just the government trying to keep us down. Additionally, that piece of paper makes it more difficult to break up.

— Derek, age 28

I met my wife four months after I swore off dating for a year. Not counting my seventh-grade attempt at dating, which involved asking someone "out" on AOL Instant Messenger only to never to talk to her in real life until we broke up two weeks later through a mediator, I had dated only one other person. At the end of my freshman year of college, after breaking up using the sparse long-distance minutes allowed by my parents' cell phone plan, I was done with dating. No one could have adequately prepared me for the culture of dating at my college.

I attended a small Bible college surrounded by cornfields in the heart of Illinois. For those of you who did not know such things as Bible colleges existed, they are schools where part of the required curriculum usually includes a class like "Hebrew History and

Literature" or "Life of Christ II." Thanks to the heightened spirituality of students, Bible colleges also tend to foster a unique atmosphere in which to search for love. Not unlike isolated wildlife environments on the Galapagos Islands or Madagascar, Bible colleges slowly evolved their own dating cultures apart from the rest of the world.

Our dating imaginations had been formed by classics of Christian subculture like *I Kissed Dating Goodbye* and *Every Young Man's Battle*. Slogans like "Ring by Spring" or "Getting an M.R.S. Degree" were the norm. Friends often tossed around the language of *soulmate* or *the one* without trying to be ironic. It was not uncommon to hear guys say, "I'm just looking for a Proverbs 31 woman," which is an expectation no actual woman could possibly meet. We would often start and end relationships the same way, bringing God into the equation and saying things like "I think God wants us to date" or "I think God wants us to see other people." Some would even save their first kiss for their wedding day. If this entire paragraph feels completely foreign to you, you're not alone.

It was on that island that I fell in love with my wife. Then we moved back to the mainland, where the dating culture could not be more different. Since I could no longer consider myself one of the natives, I had to study them in the way of an anthropologist trying to understand foreign mating rituals. Meeting someone on a dating app seemed to be the norm. The language of "hook up" meant more than it used to. It was not uncommon for people to go on multiple dates with different people in the same week. While my friends from college were getting married before they were old enough to drink alcohol, my friends in Pittsburgh were single into their late twenties or early thirties. People didn't "save themselves" for their third date, much less their wedding day. It could not have been more different than the world I had known during my own college years.

In *Modern Romance*, comedian Aziz Ansari and sociologist Eric Klinenberg argue that the modern search for love is radically different from anything else in history. In the introductory chapter, they write,

> A century ago people would find a decent person who lived in their neighborhood. Their families would meet and, after they decided that neither party was a murderer, the couple would get married and have a kid, all by the time they were 22. Today people spend years of their lives on a quest to find the perfect person, a soul mate. The tools we use on this search are different, but what has really changed is our desires and—even more strikingly—the underlying goals of the search itself.[1]

The underlying goals are different, they say. As young adults search for love, whether we are staying single or pursuing marriage, many of us are searching for something more than love. We are pioneering a barely explored relational landscape without anyone to guide us away from the dangers.

---

[1] Aziz Ansari and Eric Klinenberg, *Modern Romance* (New York: Penguin Books, 2015), 6.

It's Complicated

Augustine's relational history feels like something ripped out of the Modern Love column in *The New York Times*. After moving to the city, he entered into something like a local hook-up culture, settled into a long-term relationship, experienced pressure from his mom to break up and get married to someone better suited for him, tried out the single dad life in the months following a devastating breakup, and rebounded into another relationship while waiting to marry the woman his mother arranged for him. In short, it's complicated.

Even from his teens, Augustine had no interest in being a thirty-year-old virgin. It was during this season of his life that the "lunatic lust" (2.4) mentioned in the second chapter began to take over. When he moved to Carthage, "the center of a skillet where outrageous love affairs hissed all around me" (3.1), the lid came off. Free from the constraints of living with his highly conservative mom and the limited romantic options of his small town, he was free to explore the wide-open, urban dating scene and see what developed from there. "I wasn't in love yet," he reflects, "but I was in love with the prospect of being in love" (3.1). The young Augustine was single and ready to mingle.

After a few years of mingling, having "swooped recklessly into love" (3.1), Augustine settled down with one woman for the duration of his twenties. Although she remains nameless, her presence is felt throughout most of his *Confessions*. They had a son together named Adeodatus. Their relationship wasn't a "lawful union," but rather "a deal arising from lustful infatuation" (4.2)—not a marriage but something more akin to modern-day cohabitation. He was Velcroed to her emotionally, physically, spiritually, in every way but legally. The way he writes about her makes it obvious that he loved her, and in a different age, he might have even married her. In his socio-cultural context, though, "We love each other!" was low on the list of valid reasons to marry someone.

During his long-term relationship in his twenties, Augustine subscribed to the belief that no one could live without sex. Celibate singleness was literally unimaginable to Augustine. "I thought I would be excessively miserable," he reflects, "if I couldn't have a woman's arms around me" (6.20). In an argument with his friend Alypius, who had sex only once in his life before swearing it off completely, Augustine says, "I insisted that there was no possible way I could live a life of celibacy." Sex is too good and the urge is too strong to ever live without it, he thought. Then, after practically convincing his friend Alypius to give up on singleness and celibacy, he writes, "For me, the major factor was relationship as a habit, the habit of (temporarily) satiating an (in the long-term) insatiable lasciviousness" (6.22). Marriage was still on his mental checklist, if only as a way to legitimize his lust. An ongoing sexual relationship was the only way he could imagine being in the world.

Everything fell apart when Augustine got the call from his mom. There was an "energetic pressure" (6.23) from her to settle down and get married to someone more suitable for him. It was the "I've found you a nice, young woman from a good [rich] family who I want you to meet" conversation, except his mom ended the conversation by setting him up with an arranged marriage instead of a blind date. Although it would still be two years before Augustine could legally marry the woman his mother had chosen for him, she was *worth* the wait.

Marriage, in Augustine's day, was a family affair instead of a solo quest. It had more to do with status than love. As someone from an un-influential family in a small town, it was essential for Augustine to marry up. Marrying the woman he had been with throughout his twenties, though he loved her, would have limited his career and the potential for his family—among other complex reasons debated by scholars. Marrying a woman with the right last name meant marrying into a family with the right professional network. By the end of the conversation, his mom was calling the caterers.

With a wedding date set, Augustine's next step was to end his long-term relationship with the other woman in his life despite the fact she'd been loyal to him, and he to her, for over a decade. The breakup wrecked him. He writes,

> The woman I'd been accustomed to sleeping with was torn from my side, because she was supposed to be an obstacle to my marriage. My heart, which had fused with hers, was mutilated by the wound and I limped along trailing blood. She went back to Africa, vowing to You that she would never know another man, and leaving me with the illegitimate son she'd given birth to. (6.25)

They had given everything but wedding rings to one another, and now Augustine was sexually broken and emotionally devastated—torn, mutilated, limping, trailing blood. She must have said something like, "I swear to God, I'll never give myself to anyone again." He, on the other hand, rebounded into another relationship:

> I itched at delay, as it was two years before I could have the girl I was arranging to marry. I was no lover of marriage but instead a slave to my lust, so I secured another woman—but not a wife, to be sure. It was as if I wanted my soul's disease to be maintained unimpaired, or maybe even augmented, and conveyed into the realm of lawful wedlock, and I needed a sustained relationship to serve as a sort of escort on the journey. But that wound of mine made by hacking off the woman I'd had before wasn't healing; on the contrary, after excruciating inflammation and pain came putrefaction and growing numbness and hopelessness. (6.25)

Hoping to heal his sexual wounds, he self-medicated with more sex. Instead of healing, his open wounds festered into something even worse than before, leaving him with nothing but the vocabulary of depression. He was a single dad betrothed to a much younger woman, carrying every make and model of sexual baggage, and trying to cope with it all by hooking up with someone new—still unable to imagine the possibility of a celibate lifestyle.

Burned Out by Tinder

Single is the new married. Meg Jay, author of *The Defining Decade*, writes, "Today's twenty-somethings spend more time single than any other generation."[2] Young adults between 18 and 34 are the "fastest growing solo-dwelling population," according to Eric Klinenberg in *Going Solo*.[3] The average age of first marriages has increased from 22 for men and 20 for women in 1950 to 29 for men and 27 for women in 2015.[4] The new normal is the lifestyle that 80 percent of adults considered "sick, neurotic, and immoral" in 1957.[5] While it's often been normal to start your twenties single, it's becoming more and more likely that you will end your twenties single as well.

To be single is to be free to do what you want, how you want, when you want, where you want, and with whomever you want, without needing to ask permission from anyone else.[6] You are free to drive to the mountains for the weekend. You are free to accept a job a thousand miles away without consulting anyone. You are free to stay out until three in the morning without anyone wondering where you are. And, at least in our cultural moment, you are free to have sex with whomever you want—a freedom which 84 percent of eighteen- to twenty-three-year-olds have taken advantage of.[7]

---

[2] Jay, *The Defining Decade*, 70.

[3] Eric Klinenberg, *Going Solo: The Extraordinary Rise and Surprising Appeal of Living Alone* (New York: The Penguin Press, 2012), 5.

[4] "How is the Age at which People Get Married Changing in the U.S.?," *Overflow Data*, October 17, 2017, http://overflow.solutions/demographic-traits/how-is-the-age-at-which-people-get-married-changing-in-the-u-s.

[5] Klinenberg, *Going Solo*, 12.

[6] Jonathan Grant, *Divine Sex: A Compelling Vision for Christian Relationships in a Hypersexualized Age* (Grand Rapids: Brazos Press, 2015), 69.

[7] Grant, *Divine Sex*, 16.

I binged all ten seasons of *Friends* in 2016. (I have since deleted Netflix.) Watching the show was a way for me to understand my wife's almost daily conversational cross-references to different episodes—especially the use of the word "Pivot!" while moving furniture around our apartment. While I spent the late '90s with Monica from *Touched by an Angel*, my wife spent the late '90s with Monica from *Friends*. By the series finale, as I was still trying to make sense of my feelings about Ross and Rachel, one thing was abundantly clear: According to *Friends,* your twenties are for having as much sex as you can handle before settling down with one of the friends who was always there for you.

Friends is not an anomaly. Nearly every show we watch imagines a world in which an active sex life is normative. Except for movies produced by the Hallmark Channel, many of our romantic comedies are built on the premise that sex is just a single, inconsequential part of getting to know someone. To be single is to have sex. Singleness without sex is as unimaginable for twenty-somethings in the twenty-first century as it was for Augustine in the fourth century. If you are not having sex, some of your friends might give you a sympathetic "Aww, that's nice," while the rest of them are wondering if you're sick, neurotic, or immoral.

Living in an age free from the main social and biological consequences of sex, we have imagined that we are free from *all* consequences of sex. We don't have to worry about spending the next eighteen years raising a child because of one Friday night. We don't have to worry about what our parents or our friends will think of us. The story being sold to us is that sex is meaningless. "Only in a world where sex is meaningless," Mike Cosper writes in *Recapturing the Wonder*, "does it make sense to use the principles of video games to enable hook-ups (like Tinder)."[8] As a result, we've started to believe that sex is something as inconsequential as a side hug, even if we pretend it's not as awkward.

We act like sex is meaningless, but many of us still want it to be meaningful—in fact, more meaningful than ever. Sex is nothing and sex is everything. Without religion to make sense of our lives, we've had to search for meaning elsewhere. The less we've expected from religion, the more we've expected from sex. We've disenchanted one only to over-enchant the other, searching for God in the bedroom instead of the cathedral. We've freely stolen the vocabulary of religion and applied it our encounters with one another. Consider a few lines from Hozier's "Take Me to Church":

> If the Heavens ever did speak
> She is the last true mouthpiece
> Every Sunday's getting more bleak
> A fresh poison each week
> "We were born sick," you heard them say it
> My church offers no absolutes
> She tells me "worship in the bedroom"
> The only heaven I'll be sent to
> Is when I'm alone with you
> I was born sick, but I love it

---

[8] Mike Cosper, *Recapturing the Wonder: Transcendent Faith in a Disenchanted World* (Downers Grove: Intervarsity Press, 2017), 126.

    Command me to be well
    Amen, Amen, Amen

Or, consider the lesser known "Midnight, Hallelujah" from Jonatha Brooke:

    So you lay your hands upon me
    My whole world begins
    If love is our religion, could it be a sin?

    Stay, be my midnight Hallelujah
    Stay, be my two a.m. amen
    Stay, be my sweet, sweet revelation
    Maybe in the morning we can make amends.
    Midnight. Hallelujah.

We still want to experience something otherworldly. We still want meaning. We're just tired of looking for it in churches. In the end, we've burdened sex with more than it can bear.[9]

If the sexual revolution started in the '60s, it peaked during the last decade. Young adults who were told to believe that sex was nothing are starting to feel like it might be something more. Even without a commitment on paper, it seems that our bodies make a kind of commitment we don't realize we're signing. It's why Augustine used such brutal language when he described his breakup with a long-term sexual partner. Donna Freitas, who researched hook-up culture on college campuses, concludes, "They are acculturated to believe they are *supposed*

---

[9] Grant, *Divine Sex*, 37.

to regard sex as a casual, no-big-deal type of experience, yet many of them discover that sex is in fact a big deal."[10] Forty-one percent of us, especially women, are "profoundly unhappy" after supposedly meaningless sexual encounters.[11]

Joanna Coles, former editor of *Cosmopolitan*, says that we "pretend" that sex without commitment is fun, but in reality, "people crave intimacy, which is not easy to create in a hookup."[12] Singles still crave intimacy, meaning, love, pleasure, and fulfillment, but they are starting to wonder if the freedom of uncommitted (or under-committed) sex can meet all those needs. We're burned out by Tinder, but we keep swiping right, unable to imagine the possibility of life any other way.

High Expectations *Plus* Infinite Options

Despite the uptick in singleness, 69 percent of young adults still want to sign the papers and get married.[13] The wedding industry is bigger than ever—something my wife and I saw firsthand while we worked together as wedding photographers. In 2017, the average cost of a wedding was $33,391, with the most expensive

---

[10] Donna Freitas, *The End of Sex: How Hook-Up Culture is Leaving a Generation Unhappy, Sexually Unfulfilled, and Confused about Intimacy* (New York: Basic Books, 2013), 11.

[11] Donna Freitas, "Hookup Culture," *Q Ideas*, accessed October 11, 2018, http://qideas.org/videos/hookup-culture/.

[12] Maureen Dowd, "What's Lust Got to Do with It?," *The New York Times* (online), April 7, 2018, https://www.nytimes.com/2018/04/07/opinion/sunday/women-sex-dating-dowd.html.

[13] Jessica Bennett, "The Beta Marriage: How Millenials Approach 'I Do'," *Time* (online), July 25, 2014, http://time.com/3024606/millennials-marriage-sex-relationships-hook-ups/.

happening in Manhattan (avg. $76,944) and the least expensive in New Mexico (avg. $17,584).[14] In addition to spending more on weddings, we're also spending more time (secretly) thinking about them. In 2015, 30 percent of Pinterest boards were secret wedding boards—complete with Mason jar glasses, hues of ivory and gold, and alpacas (not a joke).[15] If singleness is the new normal, why are we spending so much of our money and so much of our secret thought-lives on weddings?

How we spend our money and what we think about most are good indicators of where we're looking for rest. Many of us are looking to marriage to do what singleness couldn't do for us. Where singleness left us wanting, we're hoping that marriage will leave us satiated. We've simply shifted the burden of fulfillment from one to the other. Just as we're searching for transcendence in sex, we're searching for significance in significant others.

Timothy Keller, author of *The Meaning of the Marriage*, says, "Never before in history has there been a society filled with people so idealistic in what they are seeking in a spouse."[16] We've drifted into

---

[14] "Couples Spend an Average of $33,391 on Weddings, Incorporating Cultural, Religious and Personalized Elements, According to The Knot 2017 Real Weddings Study," *XO Group*, February 14, 2018, https://xogroupinc.com/press-releases/the-knot-2017-real-weddings-study-wedding-spend.

[15] Julia Carpenter, "Inside the Cult of Secret Wedding Pinterest, Where Fiancés are Optional," *The Washing Post* (online), June 9, 2015, https://www.washingtonpost.com/news/the-intersect/wp/2015/06/09/inside-the-cult-of-the-secret-wedding-pinners.

[16] Timothy Keller and Kathy Keller, *The Meaning of Marriage: Facing the Complexities of Commitment with the Wisdom of God* (New York: Penguin Books, 2013), 28.

understanding marriage as the location of "emotional and sexual fulfillment and self-actualization."[17] I saw this a few years ago when I came across an article called "8 Voids in Your Life the Person You Marry Should Fill" on a website curated for a young adult audience.[18] We're willing to admit the existence of voids in our lives, including one void "we all feel but don't always know how to put into words," but without religion we end up looking to fulfill these voids in potential spouses. Psychotherapist Esther Perel, in a TED Talk from 2013, summarizes this new set of expectations on a spouse, saying,

> Marriage was an economic institution in which you were given a partnership for life in terms of children and social status and succession and companionship. But now we want our partner to still give us all these things, but in addition I want you to be my best friend and trusted confidant and my passionate lover to boot, and we live twice as long.
>
> So we come to one person, and we basically are asking them to give us what once an entire village used to provide: Give me belonging, give me identity, give me continuity, but give me transcendence and mystery and awe all in one. Give me comfort, give me edge. Give me novelty, give

---

[17] Grant, *Divine Sex*, 21.
[18] Paul Hudson, "Partners in Crime: 8 Voids in Your Life the Person You Marry Should Fill," *Elite Daily*, June 9, 2015, https://www.elitedaily.com/dating/partner-you-marry-fill-voids/1059687.

me familiarity. Give me predictability, give me surprise.[19]

When someone says it out loud, we start to get a sense of just how much we're asking of one person and it starts to feel a bit insane. If we need two hands to count the voids in our lives, we might need a therapist before we need a spouse.

Throw in the myth of endless options and you have a recipe for disaster. If this person can't meet my needs, maybe the next person can. If this person can't make me happy, maybe the next person will. Within seconds of realizing that a lover won't be able to fulfill us, we can be searching a dozen different dating apps for someone who can.

Can you imagine marrying someone who lives within walking distance of your parents' house? For most of history, your options for a spouse were limited to the children of people your parents knew. It was the cobbler's kid, your second cousin once removed, or your next-door neighbor. As recently as 1932, one-third of the five thousand married couples interviewed in Philadelphia had lived within five blocks of each other before getting married.[20] Instead of looking in a wider and wider radius for the best person, people were willing to settle for someone who was good enough.[21]

---

[19] Esther Perel, "The Secret to Desire in a Long-Term Relationship," filmed in February 2013 at TEDSalon NY2013, https://www.ted.com/talks/esther_perel_the_secret_to_desire_in_a_long_term_relationship?language=en. I first came across this in Ansari and Klinberg, *Modern Romance*, 25.

[20] Ansari and Klinenberg, *Modern Romance*, 14–15.

[21] Ibid., 22.

Compare that with our modern situation. The whole world is your neighborhood. There are hundreds of websites for people of every niche to meet one another: cat-lovers and dog-lovers, Christians and Jews, people who L.A.R.P. (that's "Live Action Role Play" for the uninitiated) and people who want nothing to do with L.A.R.P. I've learned that "the Internet" is the most likely response to asking a couple how they met. Even my dad and step-mom, who are both widowers, met on an online dating platform called Christian Cafe when online dating was still in its Wild West phase—barely any rules, no background checks, and compatibility algorithms that were still in beta testing. As one of my dad's friends said to him back then, "What kind of woman are you going to meet on the Internet?!"

Oh, how the world has changed. Instead of searching a limited pool of potential mates, you might never scrape up against the bottom of the dating pool. Dating is endless salad and breadsticks at Olive Garden. It feels like there might always be someone just a little better, a little more compatible, and a little more attractive. Anglican priest Jonathan Grant, exploring this phenomenon in his book *Divine Sex*, writes:

> What if online dating makes it too easy to meet someone new? What if it raises the bar for a "good" relationship too high, while constantly dangling attractive alternatives in front of us? What if the prospect of an ever-more-compatible

mate just a click away tempts us to chase the elusive end of the rainbow?[22]

It's the Eat'n Park menu from Chapter One all over again. Instead of choosing, we opt to never choose. If you spend a decade keeping your options open, it feels impossible to settle down with one person. You want to say the "I do" of marriage, but it's too hard to say "I don't" to everyone else.

It's here, in the messy stew of high expectations and infinite options, that many of us develop a kind of cynicism about the possibility of marriage—or, at least, monogamy. "So in our society we are too pessimistic about the possibility of 'monogamy,'" writes Keller, "because we are too idealistic about what we want in a marriage partner."[23] Instead of realizing that the problem might be with our expectations, we blame the institution of marriage itself. It's why *The New York Times* can publish a series of articles on the rise of open marriages. It's why more and more authors are trying to argue that infidelity can be good for your marriage. It's why 40 percent of us think "'til death do us part" should be removed from the marriage vows. "We are a generation raised on a wedding industry that could fund a small nation," writes Jessica Bennett, "but marriages that end before the ink has dried."[24] Of course, young adults are cynical. What else would you expect from a generation who has grown up staying with mom during the week and dad on the weekends?

---

[22] Grant, *Divine Sex*, 89.
[23] Keller and Keller, *The Meaning of Marriage*, 31.
[24] Bennett, "The Beta Marriage."

Marriage without divorce and singleness without sex are outside the realm of imaginative possibility for most of us. We've rarely seen either in person, and it seems like everyone is telling us that both options are impossible, unrealistic, and even physically and psychologically unhealthy. In the end, about half of young adults choose to live in the perpetual halfway house between singleness and marriage: cohabitation.[25] Half-committed to both marriage and singleness, it's the place where we try to enjoy the benefits of marriage while retaining the freedom of singleness. In reality, we get neither. We find that living together is a revolving doorway moving just slowly enough to step into, but too quickly to step out of into marriage or back into singleness. We're stuck somewhere in a relational no-man's land secretly scrolling a dating app on our shared WiFi bill.

More than Nothing and Less than Everything

Imagine if a famous actress from a recent movie left her acting career, took vows of celibacy, and joined a convent in Connecticut. That's precisely what actress Dolores Hart did in 1963 after visiting the Abbey of Regina Laudis—a story told in the Oscar-nominated documentary *God Is the Bigger Elvis*. It wasn't a short-lived stunt to promote her next movie or an act of desperation to regain fleeting media attention. Having shared her first cinematic kiss with Elvis Presley, Dolores Hart was a film celebrity just entering into her prime. She was still in her twenties and engaged to be married, but after spending a short retreat at

---

[25] Jay, *The Defining Decade*, 91.

the Abbey, she felt called to become a nun. In one of the most poignant moments of the film, you see Dolores walking with Donald, her former fiancé, who also remained single and visited her every year until his death in 2011. Little about her decision was easy, a tension she still feels even after decades, but she maintains that it was worth it.[26]

It was a story like Dolores' that grabbed Augustine's own imagination. Still unable to comprehend a life of singleness without sex, he met by chance with Ponticianus—a committed Christian who served in the emperor's palace. As they spoke with one another, the conversation turned toward Anthony of Egypt and the monastic life. Neither Augustine nor his friend Alypius had ever heard of Anthony or the possibility of whole communities of people living without attention to career or sex life. Ponticianus told them about how two of his own military friends "caught the spark" after encountering Anthony's story and left their own promising careers and betrothals (8.15). As Augustine listened to Ponticianus' story, he felt as if God had ambushed him, reflecting later,

> But while he was speaking, you, Master, twisted me back to yourself, catching me from behind, where I'd taken up a position in my unwillingness to pay any attention to what I was. You stood me firmly in front of my own face, so that I could see how ugly I was, how deformed and dirty, blotched with rashes and sores. I saw, and I shuddered with disgust, but I had nowhere to

[26] I first heard about this documentary in a lecture James K.A. Smith delivered at Robert Morris University in 2015.

make off to. If I so much as tried to turn my gaze away from myself, there Ponticianus was, telling that story of his, and you again confronted me with myself and forced me to look, so that I would find my sin and hate it. I knew it, but I tried to pretend I didn't; I tried to squelch any awareness of it, and to forget. (8.16)

Augustine's imagination, once closed to the possibility of celibacy, had been irreversibly opened, and his self-justification for his promiscuous lifestyle had been exposed by a carefully-crafted true story.

In addition to these stories of celibate singleness, I could also tell stories of marriages built not only on algorithmic compatibility but on covenants. I could tell stories of couples who exchanged promises to one another in their twenties and kept those promises until death did them part. I could tell stories of arguments and difficulties that might have tempted some couples to look for bliss elsewhere, but they instead chose to stick with one another. I could tell stories of spouses who stayed with husbands or wives after terrible car accidents or diseases made them shells of their former selves, able to contribute nothing to the marriage except their physical presence, marred and faded.

For those of us with small imaginations, these stories force us to grapple with an alternative to the stories of marriage and singleness we've been told our whole lives. As with Augustine, our self-justifications are exposed, and we're forced to ask, "How is that even possible?" If you're single, how could you possibly live without sex? If you're pursuing marriage or already married, how could you live without needing this one person to fulfill every longing within you?

Jesus himself was thirty-something and single. To be 30 and single in our culture is difficult, but to be 30 and single in first-century Jewish culture was almost unheard of. He was a single man living in a culture that defined a chunk of your value by whether you had children and grandchildren. Can you imagine the pressure he might have felt from his mom whenever he came home? Perhaps the conversation went something like, "Jesus, the miracles are great—especially the whole water into wine thing. We always knew you had potential for great things, but we're concerned that you haven't found a wife yet. Your younger brothers are getting married and your relatives are asking questions. I met a nice young woman of marriageable age at a well in the suburbs last week. Let me know if you want me to introduce the two of you [*mom wink*]." Nonetheless, Jesus never married and died a virgin.

Despite his lack of experience with sex or marriage, Jesus was an expert in the contours of life under God's reign. In Matthew 19:3–12, starting from a question about divorce, Jesus unpacks a better vision for singleness and marriage:

> And Pharisees came up to him and tested him by asking, "Is it lawful to divorce one's wife for any cause?" He answered, "Have you not read that he who created them from the beginning made them male and female, and said, 'Therefore a man shall leave his father and his mother and hold fast to his wife, and the two shall become one flesh'? So they are no longer two but

one flesh. What therefore God has joined together, let not man separate." They said to him,
"Why then did Moses command one to give a cer-
tificate of divorce and to send her away?" He said
to them, "Because of your hardness of heart Moses allowed you to divorce your wives, but from
the beginning it was not so. And I say to you:
whoever divorces his wife, except for sexual immorality, and marries another, commits
adultery."

The disciples said to him, "If such is the case of
a man with his wife, it is better not to marry."
But he said to them, "Not everyone can receive
this saying, but only those to whom it is given.
For there are eunuchs who have been so from
birth, and there are eunuchs who have been
made eunuchs by men, and there are eunuchs
who have made themselves eunuchs for the sake
of the kingdom of heaven. Let the one who is able
to receive this receive it."

When we think about Christianity, many of us think
only about its seemingly antiquarian, unrealistic
rules about sex. When Jesus set the boundaries for
singleness and marriage in this passage, though, his
focus was not on the rules themselves but on the better vision for singleness and marriage those rules
were intended to cultivate.

To the Pharisees, Jesus gives a better vision for
marriage. Pharisees knew the Jewish law better than
anyone else and often tried to trap Jesus with difficult
questions. In this scene, they were using an Old Testament command that permitted divorce in specific

cases as a basis for their vision of marriage—missing the heart of the law. Jesus, wanting nothing to do with their interpretation of the law, went all the way back to Genesis to paint a picture of what marriage was always meant to be.

Rather than a temporary living arrangement, Jesus defined marriage as becoming "one flesh" with another person. Marriage is about more than filling a void in your life, being happy, or even being in love. It's a lifelong union between a man and a woman, cemented in the union of our physical bodies. Sex belongs in the context of vows because sex is the most powerful uniting force on earth. Something happens when two people enter into a sexual relationship with one other that transcends the two people themselves. Keller writes, "The Bible says don't unite with someone physically unless you are also willing to unite with that person emotionally, personally, socially, economically and legally."[27] It's why divorcing a spouse, or even breaking up with a sexual partner, often feels more like the flesh-ripping language Augustine used in his *Confessions* than the language of liberation.

To the disciples, then, Jesus gives a better vision for *singleness*. After Jesus reimagines marriage, the disciples throw their hands up and say, "If such is the case of a man with his wife, it is better not to marry." If marriage is hard, maybe it would be easier to just stay single your whole life. If there is no escape hatch, maybe it would be better to just never enter into marriage in the first place.

---

[27] Keller and Keller, *The Meaning of Marriage*, 256.

In response, Jesus starts talking about eunuchs. You can almost hear the record scratch when he brings eunuchs into the conversation. For a variety of voluntary and involuntary reasons, eunuchs were committed to singleness without sex for their entire lives. To live the single life is to live in a way similar to a eunuch, Jesus says. Marriage and singleness are difficult in their own ways. Singleness is not a method for keeping your options open, a way to sleep with whomever you want, or a strategy for pursuing your own professional goals without someone holding you back. It's the life Jesus himself chose to live, "dislodging our assumption that having sex is necessary to be truly, fully alive."[28] If his vision of marriage teaches us that sex is more than nothing, his vision of singleness teaches us that sex is less than everything.

Jesus and Paul, who were both single, explain that singleness without sex is a gift to be received. Paul, in a letter to a church confused about sex, writes,

> Now as a concession, not a command, I say this. I wish that all were as I myself am. But each has his own gift from God, one of one kind and one of another. To the unmarried and the widows I say that it is good for them to remain single, as I am. But if they cannot exercise self-control, they should marry. For it is better to marry than to burn with passion. (1 Cor. 7:6–9)

---

[28] Wesley Hill, *Washed and Waiting: Reflections on Christian Faithfulness and Homosexuality* (Grand Rapids: Zondervan, 2016), 95.

Both marriage and singleness are viable options—both gifts!—for living in the world. Both have their own inherent difficulties. Both have their own advantages. Both remind us that sex is far more than nothing but still far less than everything.

These alternative visions for love are available to all but only achievable by those who are living—or loving—from rest rather than looking for rest. During what he called "the most difficult period of his life," Henri Nouwen kept a secret journal which he eventually published under the title *The Inner Voice of Love.* In the opening line, he writes, "There is a deep hole in your being, like an abyss. You will never succeed in filling that hole, because your needs are inexhaustible."[29] Though this line erupted out of the end of a close friendship, he could just as easily have been writing to those who are searching for rest in either a sexually active single life or an emotionally fulfilling marriage.

You were made for God, as Augustine reminds us, and inexhaustible needs can be met only by an inexhaustible God. The pleasure, the fulfillment, the intimacy, and the love we seek in sexual flings and holy matrimony will never permanently satisfy. With God, there is "fullness of joy" and "pleasures forevermore" (Ps. 16:11). The love of a husband or wife is a window through which we can feel the beginnings of the unending, self-giving love of God as revealed in Jesus Christ (Eph. 5:21–33). God *knows* you—your unmet potential and your annoying idiosyncrasies, your wildest hopes and your darkest secrets—and he

---

[29] Henri J.M. Nouwen, *Inner Voice of Love: A Journey through Anguish to Freedom* (New York: Image Books, 1996), 3.

still *loves* you (1 Cor. 13:12). There is a wedding still to come, which will put all our hipster barn weddings to shame (Rev. 19:6–8; 21:1–5). As you have searched for someone to notice you, God is there giving you all the attention in the world, waiting for you to look in his direction.

When you find rest in God, ordering your whole life around him, you are free to be single or pursue marriage *differently*. To reference the quote from earlier in this chapter, living from rest changes the "underlying goals of the search itself" by shrinking them back into proportion. You are free to live without sex if that's how God calls and enables you. You are free to love someone else without being wrecked by every failure to return that love. You are free to marry someone who is good enough rather than the incarnation of the gods. You are free to live in a way that points beyond your singleness or your marriage. Wesley Hill, one of my seminary professors, summarizes,

> Whether by giving it up in celibacy or by enjoying it in marriage, Christians want their sex to be a sort of pointer or window into the lavish, rapturous, closer-than-kissing love that God has for humanity, the love that God showed when he gave up his body and his life for us on the cross.[30]

Knowing this reality frees you to be hopeful in a culture cynical about the possibility of singleness without sex and marriage without divorce. It frees you

---

[30] Wesley Hill, "Sex for Christians: Self-Giving and Self-Sanctifying," *Patheos*, October 7, 2016, http://www.patheos.com/topics/spirituality-of-sex/sex-for-christians-wesley-hill.

to search not just for someone to love you but for someone you can love unconditionally.

Rather than get married, Augustine felt uniquely called to the celibate and single life—a call that seemed like an unrealistic "hardship" when he had witnessed it in his pastor in Milan (6.13). When Augustine found rest in God, his unquenchable "yearning for sex" was made somewhat manageable (8.13). After God broke through his resistance and he experienced the transformation of his desire referred to in the second chapter in his book, he writes,

> You turned me to you, so that I would pursue neither wife nor any other hope in this world, but would stand on the measuring rod of faith, as in the vision you had given me so many years before. You had turned [my mother's] mourning into a joy much more fertile than she had wished for, and much more precious and pure than she had sought from grandchildren of my body. (8.30)

After turning to God, Augustine finally felt free from the grip of "relationship as a habit" (6.22) and free to pursue a previously unimaginable life of celibacy— even if his other writings make it obvious that he *might* have overcorrected.

To live from rest does not mean you are free from struggle. To be faithful, in either your marriage or your singleness, is hard. None of the Christians I know who have chosen to be single and celibate have ever said, "Easiest thing I've ever done." Neither have any of the couples who remained married well into old age. Celibate singleness does not mean your sexual urges evaporate. Marriage does not mean the temptation to lust vanishes. No one who has ever decided to say *no* to what everyone else is saying *yes* to did so without experiencing any kind of resistance. Both vocations are glorious and difficult.

When you are at rest, though, you are free to live "for the sake of the kingdom of heaven," as Jesus said to his disciples, in either your singleness or in searching for a spouse. You are freed into a different priority than your relationship status. You are free to "seek first the kingdom of God and his righteousness" (Matt. 6:33), which means pursuing what he wants for the world and what he wants for you. Who you marry or don't marry is secondary to what you live from and what you live for.

SEARCHING FOR WORK

I saw that the church was full of people going their various ways, but I was unhappy with what I was doing in the world of time, and it was a great burden to me. I was no longer on fire with the avarice that had been usual for me, when the hope for officeholding and money made me willing to endure the quite heavy servitude I've described.

– Augustine, *Confessions* (8.2)

I have a four-year college degree and I couldn't even get a job as a barista.

– Amber, age 24

After graduating with a degree in intercultural studies, I moved back to my hometown—a few streets down the hill from where my parents lived. Not using my education in the way I anticipated, I split my week between being a pastor for young adults and an employee at a used bookstore. The store had all the expected quirks: a friendly calico cat named Diamond, a bust of Mozart staring down at you from above the cookbooks, more romance novels than you knew existed, hidden passageways behind the bookcases, and at least one patron who would often ask me where we kept our books about earthworms. It was there that I learned the kind of life lessons you can only learn at a part-time job.

For example, I learned that bats like to winter in warm, dark basements among the nonfiction paperbacks. Once, when I was reaching for a book, I felt a sharp pinch on my right pinky. What I thought was an exposed nail ended up having a foxlike face, a furry body, and wings—the look of something you would normally see behind double-paned glass in a zoo. In a moment of adrenaline, I captured the bat in a Styrofoam cup and showed it to my manager, who told me to get it out of his sight. Only later did I realize that the most common way to get rabies is from contact with a bat. It's been five years, and I'm still alive.

I also learned that your bookstore cat's "tumor" might not actually be a tumor. I opened the store one morning to find an unfinished dinner, piles of books everywhere, and no cat to be found. It looked like a scene straight out of *C.S.I.* When I turned on the computer, still trying to put together what happened there the previous night, there was an article left on the screen with the title: "How to Help a Cat Give Birth (With Pictures)." With that clue in mind, I went searching for either my boss or the cat, hoping that if I found one I might find the other. Through the half-open door to the apartment upstairs, where my manager lived, I heard the sound of multiple tones of *meow* and one tone of snoring. When I ventured inside, I found my manager asleep on the floor and two kittens roaming wide-eyed around a hastily created playpen.

At other part-time jobs, I learned that mannequins need a sponge-bath every few years, used espresso grounds can be made to look like brownies, and "husky" was *never* lingo for cold-weather clothing. And, from all of my part-time jobs, I learned what I do not want to do for the rest of my life. Many young adults can point to a moment like that in a part-time job, a moment when they thought to themselves, *I do not want to do this forever.* Knowing what you don't want to do is one thing. Knowing what you want to do is something altogether more difficult.

C's still get degrees, but degrees do not still guarantee full-time jobs. Many of us have grown up surrounded by inspirational posters with pictures of kittens saying something like *Follow your dreams!* or *You can be anything you want to be!,* only to find out those cats knew nothing about the job market. Even for those of us who do manage to get full-time jobs, there is no promise that the job will still be in existence a few years from now. Nearly half of jobs are susceptible to automation, which is to say, in short, that *robots are taking over the world.*[1] If the threat of robots wasn't enough, every week a new article runs laps on our social media feeds with a title like "17 Reasons I Quit My Job to Do What I Love (and Why You Should, Too)." Then we look around and many of our friends seem to be working their dream jobs—as seen through an Instagram filter.

Within this swirl of bad advice and disappearing options, the kindergarten exercise of imagining what we want to be when we grow up takes on a terrifying

---

[1] "Lifelong Learning is Becoming an Economic Imperative," *The Economist,* online, January 12, 2017, https://www.economist.com/special-report/2017/01/12/lifelong-learning-is-becoming-an-economic-imperative.

urgency. We're restless and searching for work, hoping that the right job will give us the rest we're longing for. As my sister told me on the phone last week, "I'm grown up, but I still don't know what I want to be when I grow up." She has a full-time job.

Not Everyone Can Make it in Rome

For Augustine, the only way out of a small town like Thagaste was getting the best education available—the one in the right school district, the one with the award-winning professors, and the one with the best pipelines to Ivy League schools. His parents, especially his dad, leveraged their networks to set him up for success, caring less about the kind of person he became and more about whether his public speaking skills were at the top of his class. If he maintained a 4.0 GPA and scored well on his SAT, all was well.

In his late teens, he transitioned into the Roman version of higher education away from his parents in the city of Carthage. He studied the art of oratory or rhetoric, which biographer Peter Brown calls the "ideal product" of the kind of education he received.[2] Looking back on this season of his life, Augustine reflects with tongue in cheek, saying, "Among these persons I was, at my impressionable age, studying books about oratory, an art in which I longed to be prominent, with the execrable goal of producing a lot of hot air for the delectation of human fatuity" (3.7). If there was ever a definition of Twitter, that's it.

---

[2] Peter Brown, *Augustine of Hippo: A Biography* (Los Angeles: University of California Press, 2000), 24.

As his skills developed, Augustine and his friends entered all kinds of speaking contests. He writes, "On the one side, we ran after the inanity of public acclaim, and went for nothing less than applause in the theater, for wrangling over poetry prizes, for literary Olympiads at which you might be crowned with grass clippings" (4.1). He wanted the kind of achievements moms love telling all your relatives about in their annual Christmas letters. Even though these contests were a never-ending cycle of "itches and cravings" (4.1), Augustine enjoyed all the attention he was getting out of them. If he'd had a social media account, it would have probably been filled with things like "#humbled to receive the poetry award (again!)."

During this stage of his life, Augustine began his teaching career and started writing his first book. But Carthage was no Rome. If you wanted to succeed in oratory, your dream was to work in Rome—the New York of Augustine's world.[3] When someone told Augustine about an opportunity there, he didn't hesitate.

Like many young adults, Augustine's search for a job was guided by a bundle of mixed motives. He explains his motives, writing,

> My reason for going to Rome wasn't the greater earning power or the greater prestige promised me by the friends who were recommending the move—though that sort of thing, at the time, also had a hold on my mind; rather, the biggest reason, and almost the only one, was that I kept hearing that there the young men pursued their

---

[3] Brown, *Augustine of Hippo*, 55.

> education more peacefully and were kept in
> check by a better regulated, more restrictive
> mode of instruction. (5.14)

He was guided by the possibility of the perfect career, the career that Carthage had not been able to deliver. He was also aware that moving to Rome meant more money alongside other less tangible benefits. Finally, he knew Rome was the place to be if you desired to be influential and well-known. Better students, bigger paychecks, and more followers. It's obvious why all his friends encouraged him to move there. It was the opportunity of a lifetime.

In the end, living in Rome was one of the most miserable years of Augustine's life. It was nothing more than another resume-building year in a career he did not want to retire doing. He traded one set of problems in Carthage for another set of problems in Rome. From within his extensive professional network, someone recruited him for a cushy job as "head rhetoric teacher" in Milan (5.23). It would be his third career opportunity in as many years, but his motives had yet to change. He still had an "open-mouthed fixation" on "professional distinctions" and "money making" (6.9), but he was beginning to grow uneasy about whether finding the right job could give him rest.

La La Land Is a Lie

Augustine's motives in searching for work are not too far off from our own. He was guided by the promise of a perfect career, the hope of a bigger paycheck, and the potential for greater influence and fame. As we think about what to do with our own lives, we ask questions like: *Which job will make the most (or, at the very least, enough) money? Which one will make me more widely known? Which one will give me the most influence? Which one will look the best on my resume? Which one will make me feel happy and fulfilled? Which one will make me the most successful?* We might never ask any of these questions out loud, but often they are swirling around just below the surface of our conscious decision-making.

Some of us are motivated primarily by the pursuit of fame—a pursuit closely linked with the pull of achievement. If this is you, you might be wondering, *Which career path has the most potential to make me well-known, important, or famous?* It could be fame within a small group of friends or family, fame within your professional field of interest, or fame across an even wider audience. In an age of reality television and the Internet, an age when seventeen-year-olds are winning gold medals in the Winter Olympics, fame feels more attainable than ever. In fact, a fifth of us secretly hope to become famous.[4] The secret is out.

There was a minute when my brother and I thought we were famous. After appearing on *Late Night with Conan O'Brien* in 2007 as a band called Rocket Me Nowhere, we half-expected this to be the start of our journey to stardom. As we left Rockefeller Center, a few people asked me for an autograph, which, upon reflection, I am certain decreased the value of whatever it is that I autographed. Then, the

---

[4] "New Research Reveals the Great Lengths Millennials are Willing to Go for Fame," *ClapIt*, January 19, 2017, http://clapit.com/press/the-new-dream-job/.

next day some other teenagers came up to us at the airport. (We had carefully placed our guitars near us so that people might think we were a big deal.) We asked if they saw us on NBC last night. They did not, nor did they care. They had come over to show us a video on their flip-phones in which for five seconds you can see them in the crowd on MTV's *TRL*. In that moment, I realized that neither we nor these teenagers were nearly as famous as we felt.

Some of us don't care about fame as long as we become financially successful. If this is you, you might be asking yourself, *Which job will make me the most money or, at the very least, provide me with a bit of financial security?* You might be thinking, *If I could just make enough money, everything would be okay.* Not all of us want a six-figure salary, but many of us— especially those of us with six-figure college debts— would like to make a little bit more than minimum wage.

Wealth, like fame, seems more within reach than ever. Mark Zuckerberg invented Facebook in his twenties and is worth over 60 billion dollars in his thirties. Bobby Murphy and Evan Spiegel, the twenty-something co-founders of the company behind Snapchat, were *already* billionaires in their twenties. I know young adults who graduated from college in the same year I did and have already achieved the status of "independently wealthy," a term I had to look up the first time I heard it. (I'm not independently wealthy.) There are young adults in my city who make more money in a month than I make in a year.

As I grow older, I have noticed the financial motivation bubble up to the surface more often. My wife and I live in a small, third-floor apartment in an old house. The roof develops a substantial leak at least once a year and the back door lets in nearly as much cold air when it is closed as when it is open. We drive a Volvo that is as old as current high-school seniors. A job that makes a comfortable income with healthcare benefits sounds more appealing than ever, especially with a new baby in the house. I don't need sixty billion, but often it feels as if sixty thousand might do the trick.

Finally, a motive I hear from young adults more and more is the longing for a fulfilling career. When asked about their top priority, 57 percent of millennials said they wanted to do something they found "enjoyable" or to feel like they are "making a difference."[5] If this is you, you might be thinking to yourself, *Which job will make me feel the most fulfilled or the most happy?* While most of us do not actually know what it would look like to work a fulfilling career, many of us are confident that our current jobs do not fit the criteria. After reading *Eat, Pray, Love*, my friend Amanda decided that her current job was unfulfilling and that she needed to do something more interesting like selling snow cones in Honolulu. Many of us have had a moment like that.

This feeling is compounded by trite and unhelpful advice like, "Do what you love and the money will follow." According to this proverb, the fulfilling job will also be the financially successful one. This advice,

---

[5] Gillian B. White, "Millennials in Search of a Different Kind of Career," *The Atlantic*, online, https://www.theatlantic.com/business/archive/2015/06/millennials-job-search-career-boomers/395663/.

unoriginal as it is, usually comes from people who did what they loved, experienced financial success, and got a book deal out of it. If you read the autobiography of a successful person, especially if they are still relatively young, it will probably follow this pattern: chapter about how they were wasting their lives at a minimum-wage job, chapter about how they quit and started pursuing their dream, chapter about the struggle of trying to make it in their dream job, a few chapters about how they made it, and some chapters of advice for the rest of us. No one gives book deals to the 99 percent of us who try this advice only to discover that it doesn't work.

If you have seen *La La Land*, you have seen this narrative play out against the background of catchy musical numbers. It's the story of Mia and Sebastian, two young adults who are living in Los Angeles trying to pursue their dreams. Mia works as a barista on a film studio lot, but she spends the rest of her time going to auditions in pursuit of her dream to be an actress. Sebastian plays piano standards to an unappreciative restaurant audience and, later, plays keyboard for an '80s cover band. But what he really wants to do is open his own jazz club. Even though their love story does not work out, both end up doing what they love. A movie about all the other young adults in Los Angeles who moved there only to move back to their hometowns three years later crushed, frustrated, and depressed would probably not have had the same effect.

But, even if we say that we do not care about being famous, financially successful, or fulfilled, many of us feel the pressure to at least appear famous, financially successful, and fulfilled. We are afraid of looking like a failure. We live for "likes." Even if I hate my job, I want it to look like I love my job. Even if it would be cheaper to move further out of the city, we take the financial hit to appear like everything is awesome. We curate our social media feeds with the best of what is happening in our lives, but as we scroll, we compare the best of what is happening in everyone else's lives to the worst of our own.

That Moment When the Neighborhood Drunk Looks Happier Than You

The quarter-life crisis is the new midlife crisis. If you haven't had one yet, it's probably coming soon. In fact, 70 percent of twenty-five- to thirty-three-year-olds claim to have one.[6] So, unless you're the lucky 30 percent who sail through their twenties while all your friends are drowning in uncertainty and self-doubt, what you're experiencing is normal.

For some of us, it's that moment when the promises of fame, financial security, and fulfillment fail to deliver the rest we're searching for. As all our favorite Disney Channel stars know, fame fades. The gap between your income and your expenses, if there even is a gap, never feels wide enough. Feelings of fulfillment rise and fall depending on the day, and there never seem to be enough "likes" to bury the feelings of inadequacy we each feel. In an oft-quoted comment, Jim Carrey said, "I wish everyone would get

---

[6] Blair Decembrele, "Encountering a Quarter-Life Crisis: You're Not Alone . . ." *LinkedIn*, November 15, 2017, https://blog.linkedin.com/2017/november/15/encountering-a-quarter-life-crisis-you-are-not-alone.

rich and famous and do everything they ever dreamed so that they would know that it's not the answer." Whatever sense of rest these things give us is momentary and leaves us even more restless than before.

Others of us experience a quarter-life crisis when, no matter what our motivations are, we find ourselves stuck in jobs we hate. We never even had the chance to experience the inadequacy of fame, achievement, wealth, or fulfillment. It's that moment when, after completing a college degree, you're still at the Dairy Queen where you've been employed since you were old enough to drive. It's that moment when your college debt payment is higher than your paycheck. It's that moment when you're 27 and you still can't find a job that can get you out of your old bedroom—the one with the Ken Griffey Jr. or *High School Musical* poster still on the wall (or both, I'm sad to say, if you're me). It's that moment when you find out no one wants to hire a twenty-two-year-old with a degree in eighteenth-century French literature and a minor in zoology. It's in these moments, when anxiety and fear and uncertainty and restlessness hit us with full strength, that we start to question whether a job can ever give us what we really want.

The quarter-life crisis is not as new as millennial-haters make it out to be. While Augustine was living and working in Milan, he had an experience that completely destabilized his plans for what he wanted to do with his life (even if, due to differences in life expectancy, it might be nearer to a third-life crisis). He had a killer career and was preparing to deliver a speech in praise of the emperor—the ultimate resume-building activity—to win the approval of everyone else who was trying to fake it until they could make it. Yet, trying to prepare this speech was filling him with a paralyzing anxiety. He writes, "My heart was issuing furnace-blasts of anxiety over this assignment, and seething with the fever of the obsessive thoughts disintegrating me from within" (6.9). As all these fears and anxious thoughts were running wild in his head, he saw a tipsy beggar who was obviously enjoying his own life far more than Augustine was enjoying his. He writes,

> In all our kinds of effort, like the effort straining me so badly now—when my longings sharply prodded me to drag along a load of my own unhappiness that was heaped up higher and higher with the exhaustion of dragging it—we didn't want anything but to reach a state of carefree enjoyment; that beggar had beaten me to it, and perhaps we were never going to arrive. Toward what he'd achieved already—which was evidently the enjoyment of a strictly time-bound happiness—with just a tiny handful of small change he'd panhandled, I was taking a woefully winding course, advancing myself by paths that circled back on themselves. He didn't have true joy, but I with all my bids for advancement was in quest of something much less real. He was enjoying himself, no doubt about it, while I was in distress; he was carefree, while I was shaking in my shoes. (6.9)

Augustine had done all the right things. He pursued the right education. He lived in the right city. He had the right credentials. He had the right job. He had the right network. Yet, here he was having a nervous breakdown while the neighborhood drunk was having the time of his life. He was slaving away to please other people, using lies to maintain an image that would impress all his friends. He was living for a glory that would fade, a paycheck that would run out, and the perfect career that would always be running away from him.

Yet, even after realizing his friends were experiencing the same anxieties on their own career paths (6.10), he stuck the course. He felt like it would be "embarrassing" (6.19) to quit after coming so far. He had already made so much "progress" toward an elite career opportunity in "some high public office." He writes, "What more is there to wish for in this world? Plenty of powerful friends are backing us; providing that we pour our effort—a lot of effort—into one thing, we could even be granted a lower-ranking governorship" (6.19). He was too deep in the pursuit of his dream to give up now, but the chase was not as wholehearted as it was before. His original fire for making as much money as possible and for advancing in his career was going out. "I was unhappy with what I was doing in the world of time," he writes, "and it was a great burden to me" (8.2). Augustine, not unlike many of us, was haunted by the possibility that he would never find the rest he was looking for in a career.

You've Been Snared by Something Untrue

In *Infinite Jest*, David Foster Wallace tells the story of students at an elite tennis academy in the Boston area. Many of these students can think about nothing other than advancing in the national tennis rankings for their age group. In one scene, LaMont Chu and Lyle, two students at the academy, are discussing what it might be like to finally be famous enough to appear in a magazine. LaMont feels like getting in a magazine would finally give his life "some sort of meaning," even if he is not sure exactly why. This conversation unfolds:

> **Lyle:** You feel these men with their photographs in magazines care deeply about having their photographs in magazines. Derive intense meaning.
>
> **LaMont:** I do. They must. I would. Else why would I burn like this to feel as they feel . . .
>
> **Lyle:** LaMont, perhaps they did at first. The first photograph, the gratified surge, the seeing themselves as others see them, the hagiography of the image, perhaps. Perhaps the first time: *enjoyment.* After that, do you trust me, trust me: they do not feel what you burn for . . . LaMont, the world is very old. You have been snared by something untrue. You have been snared by the delusion that envy has a reciprocal.[7]

You have been snared by something untrue. In other words, LaMont is longing for an experience that he thinks the famous are constantly experiencing. Celebrities aren't feeling what he thinks they're feeling. This is as true for the pull of fame as it is for every other motivation.

---

[7] Wallace, *Infinite Jest*, 388–389.

If we're searching for fame, achievement, wealth, or meaning in our work, we have been snared by something untrue. This was the same snare that trapped Augustine and traps so many young adults like us. We've been snared by the lie that if we could just get these things, then our lives, our minds—our souls!—would finally be at rest. We could finally take a deep breath and glide through the rest of our lives. What we find instead, though, if we ever get there, is that these things can only give us a momentary, fleeting taste of a rest *much less real* than even what the neighborhood drunk was able to achieve.

Timothy Keller, in his book *Every Good Endeavor*, calls all these things "the work under the work."[8] It's the work of proving ourselves through achievement, the work of finding a sense of worth through fame, the work of attaining peace through paychecks, the work of discovering meaning in the perfect job. It's the work we are still doing even after we clock out for the evening. Wallace describes it as "worship[ing] the carrot."[9] Like a cruel master, the work under the work makes us believe that we are getting closer and closer to the carrot hanging in front of us—only to find out that the carrot takes a step forward with every step we take toward it.

In the middle of the Sermon on the Mount (three chapters of teachings by Jesus in the Gospel of Matthew), Jesus speaks directly to those of us who are chasing the carrot. He says, "For where your treasure is, there your heart will be also" (Matt. 6:21). What we

---

[8] Timothy Keller, *Every Good Endeavor: Connecting Your Work to God's Work* (New York: Penguin, 2012), 234.

[9] Wallace, *Infinite Jest*, 693.

want more than anything, whatever carrot is dangling in front of us, will direct our lives. If your treasure is achievement, you'll chase after achievement. If it's fame, you'll chase fame. And so on. Whatever you treasure will determine which jobs you're willing to take.

There's a scene in *Harry Potter and the Sorcerer's Stone* when Harry and Ron discover something called "The Mirror of Erised." When Harry peered into it, he saw a vision of himself with his parents back from the dead. When Ron stared into it, he saw a vision of himself being applauded by all his peers as hero of the quidditch team. While they thought the mirror revealed their futures, Dumbledore explained what the mirror truly did. "It shows us nothing more or less," he says, gravely, "than the deepest, most desperate desire of our hearts." It revealed their treasures, their carrots, their deepest desires.[10]

Jesus warns that not all treasures are created equal. Some are prone to the slow erosion of moth and rust; others can be stolen by thieves (Matt. 6:19). Wealth can be wiped out by a bad economy. Some treasures, like fame, can fade as soon as someone more interesting comes along. Other treasures, like an inward sense of fulfillment, act like cheap balloons that are constantly losing helium until they sink to the ground. The moment you think you've found a fulfilling job, it starts to become strangely unfulfilling. Once you win and achieve something, David Foster Wallace writes, "You must keep winning to keep the

---

[10] For further explanation, see Smith, *You are What You Love*, 10–14.

existence of love and endorsements and the shiny magazines wanting your profile."[11] The moment you stop winning, stop achieving, stop making it, you're losing ground.

If we choose the wrong treasures, treasures that are on the run, we will find ourselves in a constant state of anxiety. It's why Augustine could describe his work life as "anxieties tearing at my insides" (6.9). To those of us with anxiety tearing at our insides, Jesus says, *Don't be anxious about your life*—something many of us already tell ourselves daily to no avail. Instead of leaving it there, though, Jesus tells us *why* we do not need to be anxious about our lives. He sets us free from the snare of something untrue with something truer than we could ever hope, saying,

> Therefore I tell you, do not be anxious about your life, what you will eat or what you will drink, nor about your body, what you will put on. Is not life more than food, and the body more than clothing? Look at the birds of the air: they neither sow nor reap nor gather into barns, and yet your heavenly Father feeds them. Are you not of more value than they? And which of you by being anxious can add a single hour to his span of life? And why are you anxious about clothing? Consider the lilies of the field, how they grow: they neither toil nor spin, yet I tell you, even Solomon in all his glory was not arrayed like one of these. But if God so clothes the grass of the field, which today is alive and tomorrow is thrown into the oven, will he not much more clothe you, O

---

[11] Wallace, *Infinite Jest*, 677.

you of little faith? Therefore do not be anxious, saying, 'What shall we eat?' or 'What shall we drink?' or 'What shall we wear?' For the Gentiles seek after all these things, and your heavenly Father knows that you need them all. But seek first the kingdom of God and his righteousness, and all these things will be added to you. (Matt. 6:25–34)

Jesus answers our anxieties about work with sparrows and lilies. To those of us who are tirelessly searching after something in our work, whether it be something physical like food, drink, and clothing or something less physical like achievement, fame, or fulfillment, Jesus says, *Look around you.* Why are birds not anxious even if winter is coming? Why are the flowers not toiling even though they exhibit a beauty unlike any other? What do they know that we don't know?

Sparrows and lilies, mockingbirds and roses, orioles and sunflowers—they all know that the Father cares for them. God feeds the sparrows. God clothes the lilies. If God does this for birds which are sold two for a penny and flowers which are here today and gone tomorrow, Jesus is asking us, *Will God not care for you as well?*

I've been working a part-time job as a pastor for six years. It's not for the money or the hope of being important one day (though, sometimes, I long for that) but because it's what I feel I'm called to do. I've considered chasing opportunities that paid better or offered a better pathway to being well known. There were seasons when I had to work other part-time jobs just to make ends meet and there were seasons when even that wouldn't cut it. Yet, in the midst of financial difficulty, God provided for us without us even telling anyone about our needs. In the midst of my longing to be known, God has brought me back to rest in the fact that he knows me and loves me even in the moments when it feels like no one else cares.

We will never find in a job what we can find only in God. If we search for rest in work, rest will always be out of reach. Instead of working *for* rest, then, God is inviting us to work *from* rest—the rest that comes through reordering our entire lives around him.

Instead of chasing financial security or a comfortable life, we can rest in the good news that in Christ God will give us everything we need to live. Instead of chasing the achievement that will never be enough, we can rest in the good news that Christ has already achieved for us what we could never achieve on our own (Rom. 8:3–4). Instead of chasing the fame that will rise and fall, we can rest in the good news that we are already more loved by God than we could ever hope to find anywhere else. Instead of chasing the ever-diminishing returns of fulfillment, we can rest in the good news that God is offering us a sense of fulfillment that will never leave us thirsty again (John 4:13–14). Instead of anxieties tearing at our insides, Jesus is offering us peace that surpasses all understanding (Phil. 4:7).

After his powerful experience with the gospel, Augustine entered this "rest that forgets all kinds of work" (9.11). As he became less and less enamored with wealth, influence, and advancement, it was believing the gospel that finally did away with his search for rest in his work. Now, he was "free from the gnawing anguish around advancing [himself] toward everything [he] itched for, and acquiring it, and wallowing in it, and scraping off the scabs" (9.1). While finding rest in God does not always mean quitting your job, for Augustine it did mean finding a new line of work. His career as a teacher of rhetoric had exhausted his lungs and brought him to the edge of a nervous breakdown.[12] As he writes, "Once the vacation was over, I gave notice to the citizens of Milan that they would need to get another peddler of palaver for their students, because I'd chosen instead to serve you, and was not up to the profession I'd been in, because of my difficulty in breathing and my chest pain" (9.13). He would eventually decide to spend his life serving the church.

When we find rest in God, we are freed into a new motivation for work: *faithfulness.* This is why Jesus ended his teaching, saying, "But seek first the kingdom of God and his righteousness, and all these things will be added to you" (Matt. 6:33). Instead of seeking in our work what we can only find in God, we are free to seek what God wants in our work.

For those of us without many choices for work, faithfulness might look like working obscure, low-wage, thankless, and often unfulfilling jobs. Paul, writing to bondservants in Colossae, could say, "Whatever you do, work heartily, as for the Lord and not for men, knowing that from the Lord you will receive the inheritance as your reward. You are serving the Lord Christ" (Col. 3:23–24). If people without options can make the most of their occupations, we

---

[12] Brown, *Augustine of Hippo*, 102.

should be able to do so whether we are working our dream jobs or not.

For those of us with choices for work, faithfulness means asking different questions about what to do for a living. Keller writes, "The question regarding our choice of work is no longer 'What will make me the most money and give me the most status?' The question must be, 'How, with my existing abilities and opportunities, can I be of greatest service to other people, knowing what I do of God's will and of human need?'"[13] When we ask this question, we often discover that God's will is roomier than we previously imagined. Instead of *one* perfect job out there for us, there might be an array of options about which God says, *Just pick one.*

In the end, Jesus says, "No one can serve two masters, for either he will hate the one and love the other, or he will be devoted to the one and despise the other" (Matt. 6:24). We cannot serve, we cannot worship, we cannot love both God and money, God and fame, God and achievement—God and anything else. If we choose to love something other than God, it will not love us back. It will never give us the rest we're looking for. The carrot will always be just out of reach. God, though, is offering us something better than carrots. He's offering us a treasure that will never spoil, rot, or fade—a treasure that cannot be stolen or lost. Jesus has come to bring us the rest we will never find in work.

---

[13] Keller, *Every Good Endeavor*, 67.

THE GOD SEARCHING FOR YOU

> I beg you by our Master, Jesus Christ your son, the man at your right hand, the son of humanity, whom you strengthened as your intermediary, your intermediary and ours, too, to seek us out when we weren't seeking you—no, you sought us *so that* we would seek you, meaning your Word, through which you made everything (including me).
>
> – Augustine, *Confessions* (11.4)

I came face to face with my own restlessness on a three-and-a-half-hour drive from Nagoya, Japan to Mt. Fuji. I was in the final weeks of a summer internship with Mustard Seed Network, a church-planting network in Japan, when some friends and I decided to do the midnight hike up Mt. Fuji. As the four of us were leaving the city, we made a quick stop to pick up a recent acquaintance of ours who had decided at the last minute to go with us. Squishing myself into the middle of the backseat to make room, I had no idea that I was about to have a life-altering conversation.

Our last-minute hiking buddy was a worldwide traveler. As we drove, he recounted stories of his adventures in countries I didn't even know existed and told us of all he planned to do in the coming year— including a trek across the Pacific on his boat. His stories were hilarious and intriguing. He might not have been the most interesting man in the world, but he was at least the most interesting man in the backseat of our tiny, five-passenger Japanese car.

The more stories he told, the more I longed to live the same kind of life. Having stories like the ones he told us was the primary reason I majored in cross-cultural studies, and it was one of the reasons I was in Japan that summer. I wanted to tell the best stories at parties. I wanted to be interesting and make others jealous of my life. I wanted to have the most compelling social media feed. I wanted to appear cultured and adventurous, but also be making a difference. I wanted to be just like him. I thought his life would give me the rest I was looking for.

At a gas station, just below the switchback roads where we would begin our ascent, we stopped to fill up the tank and grab something to eat. Using what little stipend I had left, I bought a corndog, a chocolate bar, and a bag of popcorn—which, in hindsight, was a regrettable life choice. When I sat back down in the car, though, something was different. As my new friend continued entertaining us with his adventures, I was no longer enthralled like I had been before the stop. In fact, I was repulsed—not with him, but with myself.

In that moment, as I listened to our friend, God had confronted me with a vision of who I was becoming, and everything in me wanted to look away. I didn't want that life any more. I knew, with sudden and almost irresistible clarity, that his life would never give me what I was looking for. There was nothing waiting for me at the summit of Mt. Fuji that I couldn't find at the base. I had been searching for rest in all the wrong places. God had found me out, and I knew it.

Prone to Wander

Moments like what I experienced in that cramped backseat happen frequently in Augustine's *Confessions*. As mentioned in Chapter Five of this book, there's a moment when Augustine, on the verge of crumbling under anxiety, sees a drunken beggar who is far happier than himself. It destabilizes his ten-year life plan. There's another moment, as recounted in my Introduction, when his friend Simplicianus tells him the conversion story of Victorinus. It fills Augustine with hope for a different life than the one he was pursuing. Then, shortly thereafter, Ponticianus, another friend of Augustine's, tells him one final story—the same story I recounted in Chapter 4—and it completely wrecks him.

In the story, two soldiers happened across a hut containing an account of Saint Anthony's life. They read about how Anthony had left everything—wealth, fame, and friends—for life with God in the barren wilderness. Upon reading the story, the two soldiers were so moved that they decided to follow Anthony's example. They committed to leaving their career ambitions and betrothals, refusing to make excuses that might get them off the hook. After telling their resolutions to Ponticianus, who was also a soldier at the time, they went back to the hut and entered a life patterned after Saint Anthony's.

When Augustine heard this story, he was certain that something within him had changed. Speaking to God, he writes,

> You stood me firmly in front of my own face, so that I could see how ugly I was, how deformed and dirty, blotched with rashes and sores. I saw, and I shuddered with disgust, but I had nowhere to make off to. If I so much as tried to turn my gaze away from myself, there Ponticianus was, telling that story of his, and you again confronted me with myself and forced me to look, so that I would find my sin and hate it. I knew it, but I tried to pretend I didn't; I tried to squelch any awareness of it, and to forget. (8.16)

He had come face to face with his own restlessness. He could no longer make the excuses he had been making before. He could no longer lie to himself about why he was resisting Christianity. God had found him out, and he knew it.

I'm sure you could recount a moment like the one Augustine experienced while listening to Ponticianus or like the one I experienced on the drive to Mt. Fuji. It's that moment when God holds up a mirror, confronting us with ourselves, showing us how we've been looking for rest in all the wrong places. He catches us off-guard, tears down our defenses, and removes any remaining excuses. He presents us with a choice about whether we will find rest in him or keep looking for it elsewhere.

These experiences happen throughout our lives, even after we choose to find our rest in God. Restlessness has a way of sneaking up on us when we least expect it. We're "prone to wander," as the hymn says, which means that it's easy to drift back into searching for rest in answers, habits, belonging, love, work, or anything else. There's always a whisper telling us to look for joy, peace, and fulfillment elsewhere—making promises that can't be kept, painting a picture that doesn't match reality. To rest in God is to resist the urge to look for rest somewhere else.

Even as I wrote this book, I could sense the urge, hear the whisper. Maybe I would feel at rest when I finished writing the book and could finally hold a copy of it in my hands. Or maybe I would be at rest if I could sell a certain number of copies or get an endorsement from someone I admire. These thoughts creep into my unguarded heart, creating the feeling Augustine described as "anxieties tearing at my insides" (6.9). Who was I to write a book on finding rest in God when I was struggling to do it myself?

Yet God used the experience of reading Augustine's *Confessions* to remind me that none of those things will give me what I'm looking for—to, yet again, force me to come face-to-face with my own restlessness. As I wrestled with Augustine, I saw myself in him. I saw myself in his longing to be known. I saw myself in the way he thought another city would give him what he needed. Augustine was not just someone in my young adults ministry; Augustine was me.

As I identified with Augustine, I was finally able to hear the good news I had been missing along. Yes, we're searching for rest in all the wrong places and only God can give us the rest we're looking for, but there's more to it than that. Long before any of us realize how far we've wandered, before any of us realize how lost we truly are, God has already been searching for us.

The God Searching for You

In the opening scene of *The Silver Chair*, the fourth book in *The Chronicles of Narnia*, a young girl named Jill Pole is hiding from school bullies. When another student named Eustace Scrubb finds her crying, he recounts his recent adventures in the land of Narnia, a world of talking animals, dragons, and magic. Together, they start calling out the name of Aslan, even though Jill has no idea who that is, hoping that he will hear them and quickly rescue them from that terrible school.

Nothing happens. Even worse, they start to hear the bullies rounding the corner. Uncertain of what they should do to escape, Jill and Eustace run toward a door at the edge of the property. Normally, it's locked. This time, though, they discover it's unlocked. They decide to walk through it, only to find they are no longer near the bullies or the school or in England at all, but in Narnia.

Shortly after their arrival, still catching their breath from the escape, Eustace slips over the edge of a cliff. Out of seemingly nowhere, a great lion—whose identity is still unknown to Jill—rescues Eustace and takes him somewhere out of sight. Then the lion returns to take a drink from a stream. Jill, who never imagined speaking to lion, finds the courage to walk up to the lion and find out what's happening.

As she approaches the stream, the lion speaks to her and tells her about a task he has for her to complete. In fact, it is for this task that he *called* Jill and

Eustace out of their world and into his own. Confused, Jill says,

> "I'm wondering—I mean—could there be some mistake? Because nobody called me and Scrubb, you know. It was we who asked to come here. Scrubb said we were to call to—to Somebody—it was a name I didn't know—and perhaps the Somebody would let us in. And we did, and then we found the door open."

> "You would not have called to me unless I had been calling to you," says Aslan.[1]

It's easy to think that you're leading the search. That *you're* the one looking for answers, habits, belonging, love, and work; *you're* the one searching for rest in all the wrong places; *you're* the one trying to find God. It's easy to read Augustine's *Confessions* the same way, as if his own self-initiated spiritual quest carries the story along. By the end, though, it's clear that the opposite is true.

Your story, like *Confessions*, is not primarily about your search for God. It's about God's search for you. Long before you were seeking God, before you had any inkling that something wasn't right, God sought you out by sending his Son, Jesus Christ. In fact, as Augustine says, God sought you *so that* you would seek him. Through the ancient prophet Isaiah, God says to his people,

---

[1] C.S. Lewis, *The Silver Chair* (New York: Collier Books, 1980), 18–19.

> I revealed myself to those who did not ask
>> for me;
>> I was found by those who did not seek me.
>
> To a nation that did not call on my name,
>> I said, 'Here am I, here am I.'
> All day long I have held out my hands
>> to an obstinate people,
> who walk in ways not good,
>> pursuing their own imaginations (Isa. 65:1–2)

God is the initiator. He is the one who went after you. You are not the one who finds God. He is the one who finds you. As Augustine says, continuing his ongoing prayer to God, "But now, don't abandon me when I call on you—you who, before I called on you, got in ahead of me with proliferating and multifarious utterances, so that I could hear from far away and turn around, and call on you who were calling me" (13.1).

Jesus tells a story of a shepherd who leaves ninety-nine sheep to seek a lost one. The ninety-nine sheep, perhaps, don't even realize that anything is wrong, while the shepherd is on a wild hunt to track down his lost sheep before it's found by someone with more sinister motives. Jesus asks, "Doesn't he leave the ninety-nine in the open country and go after the lost sheep until he finds it? And when he finds it, he joyfully puts it on his shoulders and goes home. Then he calls his friends and neighbors together and says, 'Rejoice with me; I have found my lost sheep'" (Luke 15:4–6).

God has left everything—a wild and unpredictable move—to search for you. And he's found you. He knows exactly where you are. All that's left is for you to let him pick you up, carry you home, and throw you the craziest party you'll ever attend.

Look no further. The search is over. You can rest now.

Come to me, all you who are weary and burdened, and I will give you rest.

APPENDICES

HOW TO MAKE YOUR OWN
STICKY-NOTE *CONFESSIONS*

A ll of us want to make sense of our lives, but most of us are not capable of writing our own *Confessions*. What if we could use sticky notes instead? Using an exercise developed by Terry Walling, founder and president of Leader Breakthru, our church has helped dozens of people create their own sticky-note timelines.[1] With permission from Terry Walling and following the lead of Augustine, I want to offer a slightly adapted sticky-note timeline exercise for you.

First, gather the supplies you will need: 1) four different colors of sticky-notes (with at least two being yellow and pink), 2) a poster board cut in half, and 3) a pen.

Second, begin exploring what Augustine calls "the spacious palaces of memory" (10.12). Think of every significant person, event, or set of circumstances that you can remember—negative or positive—and write each one down on a separate sticky-note in no more than a few words. Consider the people who influenced

---

[1] © Terry Walling / Used by Permission. For more information on Leader Breakthru: www.leaderbreakthru.com. For a visual explanation, please view Terry Walling's video posted at www.leaderbreakthru.com/ transitions/post-it-note-timeline.php.

you directly or indirectly: friends, pastors, family members, authors, mentors. Consider the events that marked your life: deaths, breakups, marriages, job changes, moves, achievements. Consider the circumstances, those within your control or those beyond your control, that influenced your trajectory: childhood experiences, parental expectations, places you've lived.

Make it an exercise of prayer. Like Augustine, ask God to help you remember things you might have forgotten. As the ancient poet says, "Search me, God, and know my heart" (Ps 139:23). Augustine, exploring his own memory, writes,

> Certain things issue forth immediately; certain other things need a lengthy search, and it's as if they were being dug out from this or that obscure, neglected container; and certain other things charge at you in hordes: when you're asking and looking for something else, they rush into the open as if they're saying, "Is it maybe us you want?" (10.12)

Some memories will come to you quickly and others might require more digging. Some memories will revive pain you have suppressed, and others will reignite a forgotten joy. It's okay to add on more memories later as you think of them.

Third, with all the sticky-notes spread out on a table, identify which of the memories were painful as you experienced them. Once you identify those memories, transfer them from a yellow sticky-note to a pink one and get rid of the yellow version. For me, it's memories like the death of my mom when I was eleven-years old, discovering pornography for the first time as a junior-higher, a painful relationship in my late teens, and friends who moved away in my twenties. For Augustine, it might have been joining the Manichean cult, the death of a close friend, his year in Rome, and his breakup with his long-term partner—for starters.

Fourth, organize your sticky notes in the order you experienced them. Add a sticky-note marked "X" to the top left and bottom left corners. These notes will preserve a margin at the top and bottom of your poster board for the next steps. Then, begin adding your sticky-notes chronologically under the note marked with an "X" in the top left corner. Add them from top to bottom until you reach the "X" in the bottom left corner. Then, start a new column to the right and add sticky-notes from top to bottom again. Keep going all the way across the poster board until you run out of sticky-notes. If Augustine were making a timeline, this step might look something like this:

X			
Monica, My Mother (yellow)	Falling in Love (yellow)	Becoming a Catechumen (yellow)	Ponticianus (yellow)
Pear Tree Incident (pink)	Birth of Adeodatus (pink)	Seeing Drunk Beggar (pink)	"Pick it up! Read it!" (yellow)
Moving to Carthage (pink)	Death of Friend (pink)	Alypius/ Nebridius (yellow)	Baptism (yellow)
Reading Cicero (yellow)	Year in Rome (pink)	Betrothal and Breakup (pink)	Death of Monica (pink)
Joining the Manicheans (pink)	Moving to Milan (yellow)	The Neoplatonists (yellow)	
First Teaching Job (yellow)	Meeting Ambrose (yellow)	Simplicianus (yellow)	
X			

Fifth, using a different colored sticky-note, add no more than six chapter titles in the top margin of the poster board. (You can get rid of the space-saving sticky-note marked "X".) Think of these as chapters in your life. Augustine just referred to the different sections of his life as "books," but you can get as creative as you want to be. In my own timeline, I title the different chapters according to the major geographical moves in my life: Portland, East Tennessee, Pittsburgh, Illinois, Pittsburgh (Again).

Sixth, mark six to eight sticky-notes that represent major turning points with a small "X" in the corner of the note. Walling defines turning point as a "life-changing event or circumstance" when someone intervened in your life, a major decision was made, or a crisis occurred. For Augustine, turning points might have included joining the Manicheans, meeting Ambrose, and his experience of hearing "Pick it up! Read it!" in the garden.

Seventh, reflect on the lessons God might have been teaching you at different parts in your timeline—especially, the turning points. Use a different colored sticky-note to record some of those lessons in the margin at the bottom of your poster board. Throughout his *Confessions*, Augustine frequently points out where God was at work. Summarizing some of Augustine's thoughts on memory in Book Ten of his *Confessions*, Alan Jacobs writes,

> Through memory, Augustine explains at various points in Book X of *Confessions*, we are able to review past action and discern a variety of important themes: we can see when we were moving towards God and (conversely) when we were moving away from Him; when we discerned the good rightly and sought it properly and (conversely) when we misidentified the good and sought experiences or possessions that were bad for us; when God was calling us toward Himself, whether we heard His voice or not; and so on.[2]

Like Augustine, as you look over your story, you will be able to see God at work in places you never expected. Ask questions like: Where might God have been at work in this event? What did God teach me

---

[2] Alan Jacobs, "What Narrative Theology Forgot," *First Things*, online, August 2003, https://www.firstthings.com/article/2003/08/what-narrative-theology-forgot.

through that person? How did God draw me toward himself when I wasn't even aware of it?

Finally, share your timeline—your *Confessions*—with someone. Augustine wrote his *Confessions* not just for himself but for others. Your story contains wisdom that others need.[3] In fact, hearing you tell your story might become a major turning point in the life of someone else. It was stories told by Simplicianus and Ponticianus that left Augustine desperate for his story to end in the same way. Even though your story is still open-ended, with sticky-notes still to be added, it's never too soon to share your story with others. By allowing God to help you make sense of your own life, he will use you to help others make sense of theirs.

---

[3] Alan Jacobs, "What Narrative Theology Forgot."

HOW TO READ AUGUSTINE'S
CONFESSIONS

I like to think of *A Restless Age* as a prologue to Augustine's *Confessions* for young adults. Secondhand Augustine can still speak, of course, but he's meant to be experienced firsthand—unmediated by the opinions of someone, like myself, writing *about* him. If his book appears next to mine in Amazon's "frequently bought together" section, my job is done.

As I admitted in the introduction to this book, I struggled through *Confessions* when it was assigned in college. Except for the Bible, I was not accustomed to reading old books, choosing instead to read Michael Crichton novels. *Confessions*, written in the fourth century, qualifies as an old book. Augustine's sentences are long. His arguments are hard to follow. His social, political, and religious context is unfamiliar. He wrestles with ideas that mean nothing to me, and I cringe at his unawareness of twenty-first century political correctness. Sending you into Augustine's *Confessions*, especially if you are not much of a reader, feels like I am setting you up for a reading disaster.

C.S. Lewis, introducing another old book, says, "It is a good rule, after reading a new book, never to allow yourself another new one till you have read an old one in between. If that is too much for you, you should at least read one old to every three new ones."[1] If we only read new books, he says, we are in danger of never being challenged by ideas outside of our cultural moment. We are in danger of missing out on the delights of meeting an ancient author face-to-face and, perhaps, we are even "half-afraid" of what might happen if we do.[2] In fact, you should just read Lewis' "Introduction to Athanasius' *On the Incarnation*" instead of my own essay on the subject.

My own book, not unlike most books written this year, will be forgotten. *Confessions* will not be. It has already survived the passage of time, literature's fiercest critic, making it immune to Amazon ratings. It's difficult, yes, but there are delights hidden in difficulty, new treasures to be drawn out of what is old. Mine is your new book; now read an old one. Hopeful that Augustine's *Confessions* can do for you what it has done for millions before you, I offer a few suggestions:

First, *pay more for a good translation.* Resist the ninety-nine-cent version you can download to your phone. Up until recently, I had only read John K. Ryan's translation, which contains some wonderful turns of phrase. In the early stages of writing this book, a friend suggested Sarah Ruden's translation.

---

[1] C.S. Lewis, "Introduction to Athanasius' *On the Incarnation*." It's available online at http://silouanthompson.net/library/early-church/on-the-incarnation/introduction/.
[2] Ibid.

Her work gave new life to the book. It's colloquial, which means it sounds more like a conversation (since that's what it is!), though, in her quest to find the right words, she does choose a few words that left me scrambling for a dictionary (e.g., *multifarious*, used in the quote I referenced in the conclusion of this book, which means "many and of various types"). I wrote her a thank-you letter. It's *that* good.

Turn off everything but the lamp. Lock up your phone for an hour. Whenever you lift your eyes from reading to check a ding from your phone, you experience what psychologists call "switching costs," which refers to the time and mental energy associated with moving your attention to a new task—even if that task only takes a few seconds.[3] If you're trying to read Augustine's discussion of the *will* and find yourself checking for social media updates every few minutes, you're only proving his point. It takes undistracted attention to get into a reading groove, but once there, it's difficult to leave.

Find some running buddies. I have never run a marathon, nor do I plan on ever running one, but I know that they are easier with friends. Reading *Confessions* will feel like a reading marathon. You'll dream about quitting on every other page. You might pass out midway through Book Seven, but if you have friends who are reading it with you, you're more likely to stick with it until the end—if only to not look like the quitter. Or you'll all quit together and binge something on Netflix instead.

---

[3] Nicholas Carr, *The Shallows: What the Internet Is Doing to Our Brains* (New York: W.W. Norton and Company, 2011), 133.

Know when to slow down or speed up. There are thirteen books, but some of them will feel hopelessly confusing on your first read. It's okay to skim. Others will feel like every other sentence must be shared with everyone you know. It's okay to read those paragraphs two or three times. I suggest reading one book per week, except for Book Ten, which I suggest reading in two weeks. At this pace, you'll be able to both slow down and speed up as necessary while maintaining a sense of momentum.

Keep a Bible handy. Augustine has steeped in the Christian scriptures more than any of us. His imagination is so formed by biblical vocabulary and phrases that he cannot help but quote it. On one page, I counted fourteen separate references. Look up *some* of his biblical shout-outs as you go. Like any conversation with an expert in something, it's easy to get lost if you haven't read the same things he's read.

Be ready to stop and sing. Augustine's love for God is contagious. Reading him might do more to ignite your devotion than a typical *devotional.* C.S. Lewis is insightful on this point, saying,

> For my own part I tend to find the doctrinal books often more helpful in devotion than the devotional books, and I rather suspect that the same experience may await many others. I believe that many who find that "nothing happens" when they sit down, or kneel down, to a book of devotion, would find that the heart sings unbidden while they are working their way through a

tough bit of theology with a pipe in their teeth and a pencil in their hand.[4]

Get a notebook. As you read a section, write down what moves you. Focus more on what resonates and less on what confuses you—especially on the first read. It might be a quote that hit you right where you needed it or an experience of his you can relate to. Often, after reading a book I loved, I cannot recall a *single* thing that moved me about it. Reading more with less reflection will not do for you what reading less with more reflection will do.

Let it be strange. There will be moments in reading Augustine when you say, "What?! How could anyone believe something like that?" Suspend judgment. Sit in the weirdness. Sometimes, it feels strange because it's wrong; other times, it's because we're wrong. Again, C.S. Lewis writes, "Every age has its own outlook. It is specially good at seeing certain truths and specially liable to make certain mistakes. We all, therefore, need the books that will correct the characteristic mistakes of our own period. And that means the old books."[5] When you encounter something strange, stop and ask why. Seek first to understand.

Finally, *read it again*. I've read *Confessions* three times now. On my first reading, nothing happened. On my second reading, I was captivated by it. On my third, I was *changed*. Your experiences shape what you pay attention to. A section that meant nothing to you on your first reading might change your life on the second reading. For many years, I thought books

---

[4] Lewis, "Introduction to Athanasius' *On the Incarnation*."
[5] Ibid.

were for reading once, not realizing that surface-level riches are only a clue to the treasures that might be found on second, third, or fourth reading.

DISCUSSION QUESTIONS

Chapter 1: Searching for Answers

1. What are some of the questions that have haunted your life so far?
2. Where have you looked for answers in the past?
3. Can you recall a moment when you realized some of the answers you had believed were absolutely wrong? What was that like?
4. Are you more prone to personalize your own set of answers or to feel paralyzed by all the answers out there (or both)? Why is that?
5. How would you explain to someone else that Jesus is more than just another set of answers?

Chapter 2: Searching for Habits

1. What are some habits you wish you could change about yourself?
2. Are you more prone to trying to change those habits or trying to convince yourself that you're fine just the way you are? Why do you think that is?

3. Can you recall an experience of feeling like you wanted to change and like you *couldn't* change—at the same time?

4. What is so good about the fact that God sent his Son for us even when we felt stuck in the habits we hate?

5. What difference might it make if you were trying to change your habits *from* a place of rest in God rather than *for* rest?

Chapter 3: Searching for Belonging

1. Do you have your own story of feeling excluded from something like the Cherry Hill Drive Beanie Baby Club?

2. What has been your experience of trying to find a sense of belonging? Do you gravitate more toward loneliness or tribalism?

3. Can you relate to feelings of loneliness in your life so far? When?

4. What are some ways you've seen tribalism in your own life or in the lives of those around you?

5. How is the church good news for those searching for belonging?

Chapter 4: Searching for Love

1. Where did you see yourself in Augustine's search for love?

2. What makes searching for love complicated in our cultural moment?

3. Do you long more to be single or to be married? Why do you think that is?

4. Where have you felt pain in either singleness or relationships?
5. What difference would it make to be single or married *from* a place of rest in God?

Chapter 5: Searching for Work

1. What are some of the jobs you've worked in your life so far?
2. Where did you see yourself in Augustine's search for work?
3. Which motivation in the search for work could you relate to the most: fame/achievement, wealth, fulfillment? Why do you think that is?
4. Have you experienced a quarter-life crisis? What was that like?
5. What difference would it make to search for work *from* rest rather than *for* rest?

ACKNOWLEDGMENTS

T hank you to the fantastic GCD Books team. Jeremy Writebol, for deciding to invest in a new writer after noticing something in my original pitch. Grayson Pope, for walking me through the whole publishing process and handling my questions with grace—in addition to providing critical feedback where I needed it most. Lauren Bowerman and Aarik Danielsen, editors who are capable of drawing out the best in my writing and meticulously deleting the sub-par.

Thank you to Deanna Briody and John Bryant, two of the best writers I know, for reading early drafts of this book. Deanna, for caring more about the quality of the book than about my self-esteem. John, for letting me know that my best sentences were in all the wrong places. When each of you, at different times, told me that you already had someone in mind who needed to read this book, I was encouraged more than you could possibly understand.

Thanks to the professors who, after reading my academic writing, challenged me to keep writing. You took time to comment not only on the content of my papers but on the style. If it were not for professors like Rob Maupin, Neal Windham, Wesley Hill, Leslie Thyberg, and Phil Harrold, I doubt that I would have ever had the courage to share any piece of my writing with a wider audience.

Thanks to the young adults who attend Bellevue Christian Church. I wrote this for you. You've opened up to me about breakups and doubts and struggles and insecurities and loneliness, teaching me how to be a pastor in the process. You've endured sermons that (accidentally) lasted over an hour as I've tried to work out what the gospel sounds like in the mess of young adulthood. The insights you provided through conversations and emails gave heart to this book.

I want to say a special thanks to Commonplace Coffee (Mexican War Streets), Cyclops Cafe, and Anchor & Anvil Coffee Bar for providing me with a space to write for an hour (or three) for the price of a twelve-ounce coffee. Julien Baker, your album *Turn Off the Lights* was on repeat while I wrote Chapter Two. Sandra McCracken, your album *Songs from the Valley* is so good that I had to stop playing it when I was trying to actually get some writing done. Giant Lion, *Take Up Your Crown* was often the jumpstart I needed to start writing at 5:30 a.m. Sarah Ruden, your translation of *Confessions* made Augustine come alive and your feedback at the eleventh hour made the book better. Thank you.

Thanks to Laura Brown, Jeff Browning, Nicholas Chambers, Ezra Dulis, Chuck Gohn, Josh and Alicia Hoey, Mark Sciaruto, Amelia Shuppy, Amanda Tuttle, Jacob Williamson, and Seth Zimmerman, for providing encouragement and feedback at different points throughout the writing process. Also, thanks to the whole MERGE team this past year—Todd and Sam Ransom, Rachel Stojkovic, Alex Scott, Ryan

Hreczkosiej, Justin Langston, JJ Faltot—for frequently asking me about the book and making me believe this book might actually make a difference in the lives of real young adults.

Finally, thanks to my wife Julie and my son Levi. Julie, you got up to feed Levi and get him back to sleep when you knew I needed to write in the morning. As you listened to and read early drafts of the book, you knew when I was too insecure for critical feedback and when I was ready to hear the feedback necessary to make the book even better. I love you, and I could not have done it without you. Levi, you did nothing but press computer keys when I was trying to write, but I love you anyway and I was thankful for the reminder that no task is more important than spending time with those who will outlive this book.

ABOUT GOSPEL-CENTERED DISCIPLESHIP

You may have noticed that there are a lot of resources available for theological education, church planting, and missional church, but not for discipleship. We noticed too, so we started Gospel-Centered Discipleship to address the need for reliable resources on a whole range of discipleship issues.

When we use the term "gospel-centered," we aren't trying to divide Christians into camps, but to promote a way of following Jesus that is centered on the gospel of grace. While all disciples of Jesus believe the gospel is central to Christianity, we often live as if religious rules or spiritual license actually form the center of discipleship.

Jesus calls us to displace those things and replace them with the gospel. We're meant to apply the benefits of the gospel to our lives every day, not to merely bank on them for a single instance of "being saved." A gospel-centered disciple returns to the gospel over and over again, to receive, apply, and spread God's forgiveness and grace into every aspect of life.

GOSPEL-CENTERED DISCIPLESHIP RESOURCES

Visit GCDiscipleship.com/Books.

The Christian life is knowing God. It is not an impersonal knowledge of bare facts but one rooted in wonder at "the light of the knowledge of the glory of God in the face of Jesus Christ" (2 Cor. 4:6). It is knowing that basks in the glories of the gospel.

In *Gospel Glories from A to Z*, Kelly Havrilla works to reflect some of that glory onto each page as she connects deep biblical truths through the structure of the alphabet. Useful for both those new to the beauty of Christianity and those looking for a fresh way to grow deeper this book aims to make God's grace abundantly clear and accessible. Our hope is that this reflection will spark a desire to venture into deeper waves of gospel glories.

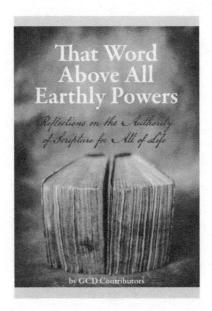

As the Protestant church celebrates the 500th anniversary of the Reformation the question of the authority and power of the Word of God for everyday life is still raised by many. Through this collection of essays, the Gospel-Centered Discipleship team seeks to demonstrate not only the rich theological implications of the authority of the Bible, but also the life-altering power of God's Word for everyday, ordinary life.

GCD's aim is to see the Word of God "make, mature, and multiply disciples of Jesus." As Martin Luther declared, "the Bible is alive, it speaks to me, it has feet, it runs after me, it has hands, it lays hold [of] me." He was announcing the power of the Bible "above all earthly powers."

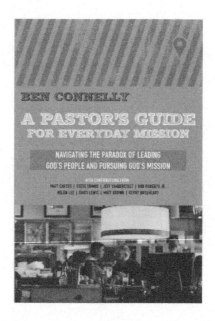

After fifteen plus years of vocational ministry, Ben Connelly had an epiphany. He had missed the great commission. He was really good at keeping Christians happy and really bad at making disciples. *A Pastor's Guide to Everyday Mission* helps those in paid ministry positions rediscover—and live—their life as God's missionaries, even as they minister to God's people.

We stand in the already and not yet. We are disciples serving between Christ's coming and his coming again. As we look backward, we see an astonishing baby boy cradled in his mother's arms and the saving life he will lead. Looking forward, we see a complete kingdom and restoration of all things. We celebrate Christmas only after grappling with the hope fulfilled and the hope still waiting.

Too often we limit the power of the gospel to its blessings for us in the afterlife. We fail to see how the power of God, which raised Jesus from the dead, fuels our day-to-day battle against sin in this life. *Renew* shows us the grace of God is able to change us now.

For those looking to break specific sinful habits and temptations as well as those looking to gain a better grasp of how a Christian grows, *Renew* speaks to the power of the gospel today.

Written as a series of letters in a gentle, conversational tone, this book is an interactive tool designed to help those in a spiritual mentoring relationship. It summarizes four areas in following Christ: the beliefs of a Christian, living like a Christian, habits of a Christian, and exploring the Bible. Jenny McGill, a ministry leader and pastor's wife, will encourage and bolster you in your Christian faith, addressing some difficult subjects in a down-to-earth fashion. Approachable and engaging, *Walk with Me* is a discipleship guide and aid to all believers, no matter how long they have walked with Jesus.

Made in the USA
Middletown, DE
02 July 2019